STEVE TERRILL

NUMBER ONE

OREGON MOUNTAIN RANGES

By George Wuerthner

COPYRIGHT © 1987
AMERICAN GEOGRAPHIC PUBLISHING ❏ HELENA, MONTANA 59604
ALL RIGHTS RESERVED ❏ TEXT © COPYRIGHT GEORGE WUERTHNER

WILLIAM CORDINGLEY, CHAIRMAN
RICK GRAETZ, PUBLISHER
MARK THOMPSON, DIRECTOR OF PUBLICATIONS
BARBARA FIFER, ASSISTANT BOOK EDITOR

This series provides in-depth
information about Oregon's
geographical, historical, cultural and
natural history subjects. Design by Len
Visual Design. Printed in Hong Kong by
DNP America, Inc., San Francisco.

ACKNOWLEDGMENTS

Many, many people assisted me in the research for this book—too many to list individually, but the personnel of the University of Oregon and Oregon State Universities, U.S. Forest Service, Bureau of Land Management, Malheur Wildlife Refuge, and Oregon Department of Fish and Wildlife all gave willingly of their knowledge and expertise. Without their help I could not have completed this book; to each, I extend my thanks. In addition, many thanks to James Monteith of Oregon Natural Resource Council for providing valuable insights to Oregon conservation issues, Dave Alt of the University of Montana Geology Department for reviewing the geology chapter, Mark Thompson and Rick Graetz at American Geographic Publishing for their support and guidance, and Mollie Matteson, who reviewed and edited the entire manuscript. Finally, I wish to thank the people throughout Oregon who shared with me their pride in and love of Oregon's mountains.

American Geographic Publishing
Box 5630 • Helena, Montana 59604
(406) 443-2842
Idaho • Montana • Oregon • Washington • Wyoming
ISBN 0-938314-30-0

CONTENTS

Oregon's Mountain Ranges

Photos, left to right: View from Mt. Hebo GEORGE WUERTHNER: Asters and Steens Mountain STEVE TERRILL: Castle Rock GEORGE WUERTHNER. **Inside front cover:** The Brothers Fault GEORGE WUERTHNER. **Inside back:** Clackamas River GEORGE WUERTHNER. **Back cover:** Garfield and Applegate Peaks PAT O'HARA. **Front cover photos,** clockwise from upper left: At Boardman State Park GEORGE WUERTHNER, Broken Top Mountain and Sparks Lake STEVE TERRILL, Lower Proxy Falls in the Cascades GEORGE WUERTHNER, Mt. Hood STEVE TERRILL, Wallowa Mountains STEVE TERRILL

CHAPTER 1

Introduction

Not all Oregon mountains are covered with lush vegetation. Above: bunchgrasses and juniper frame Smith Rocks along the Crooked River near Redmond. Right: Oregon's mountains are famous for their old giant Douglas fir forests, seen here in the Cascades by Mt. Jefferson Wilderness. GEORGE WUERTHNER PHOTOS

The most widespread mental image of Oregon is probably formed from calendars and textbooks depicting a glacier-clad Mt. Hood reigning majestically over a wilderness of giant conifers. Many people have come to believe all of Oregon is a magnificent, forested range of high, snow-covered peaks.

Such misconceptions are probably common outside of Oregon, for most travel promotion brochures focus on the dramatic Cascade Peaks and the coast, but seldom mention the rest of the state. Nevertheless, there is much more to Oregon than Mt. Hood, and its mountains in particular offer a great diversity of landscapes from the low, densely forested Coast Ranges to the sage-covered, treeless slopes of eastern Oregon's desert peaks.

The state covers some 61,599,000 acres—roughly 345 miles from the Idaho border on the east to the Pacific Ocean on the west, and 278 miles north to south. Along the northern coast are the low, heavily forested mountains of the Coast Range, while south of Coos Bay, the western face of the Siskiyou Mountains—sometimes called the Klamath Mountains—meets the sea. The rugged Siskiyous dominate the entire southwest corner of the state and arc eastward to join the Cascades by Medford.

East of the Siskiyous and the wide Willamette Valley are the state's highest and most prominent mountains—the Cascades. Formed by recent volcanic activity, many of the higher peaks like South Sister and Bachelor Butte display the classic cone shape most people associate with volcanoes. The Cascades form an imposing barrier to storm pathways and as a result mark a dramatic, climatic dividing line between the mild, wet weather typical of western Oregon and the colder, but much drier portion of the state east of these mountains.

Beyond the Cascades, stretching diagonally across the northern third of the state from Prineville to the Washington-Idaho border, are the Blue and Wallowa mountains. The Blues are composed of a number of sub-ranges including the Ochocos, Elkhorns, Strawberrys and others. Just slightly lower in elevation than the Cascade Peaks, many of these mountains resemble Rocky Mountain ranges in forest cover and wildlife, and many geographers consider them to be the westernmost outliers of the Rocky Mountains.

South of Burns and the desolate high desert valleys like Christmas Lake and Ft. Rock are the Basin and Range mountains—Oregon's least known and most isolated mountains. These widely spaced ranges such as Steens

Astoria
Saddle Mtn.
Portland
Tillamook
Mt. Hebo
Columbia Gorge National Scenic Area
The Dalles
Mt. Hood
Barlow Pass
Cape Foulweather
Newport
WILLAMETTE VALLEY
CASCADE RANGE
Mt. Jefferson
Mary's Pk.
Corvallis
McKenzie Pass
Waldport
WESTERN OR OLD CASCADE RANGE
Three Sisters
Heceta Head
Eugene
McKenzie R.
Bachelor Butte
Bend
Maury Mtns.
Florence
Oregon Dunes National Recreation Area
NEW CASCADES
Paulina Mtns.
Newberry Crater
Umpqua R.
Diamond Pk.
Coos Bay
UMPQUA VALLEY
Diamond Lk.
Mt. Thielsen
Yamsay Mtn.
Winter Ridge
Port Orford
Crater Lake National Park
Humbug Mtn.
Rogue R.
Upper Klamath
Grants Pass
Medford
Mt. McLoughlin
Gearhart Mtn.
KALMIOPSIS Wilderness
SISKIYOU MTNS.
Klamath Falls
Brookings
Whisky Pk.
Mt. Ashland

Wenaha R.
Hells Canyon National Recreation Area
Grande Ronde R.
La Grande
Enterprise
Matterhorn Pk.
WALLOWA MTNS.
Eagle Cap Pk.
Elkhorn Mtns.
Baker
BLUE MTNS.
Greenhorn Mtns.
Ochoco Mtns.
Prineville
John Day
Aldrich Mtns.
Strawberry Mtns.
Burns
Malheur Lk.
Harney Lk.
Jackass Mtns.
Steens Mtn.
Sheepshead Mtns.
BASIN & RANGE
Catlow Rim
Alvord Desert
Hart Mtn.
Beatys Butte
Pueblo Mtns.
Trout Creek Mtns.

5

Mountain, Trout Creek Range, the Warner Mountains, and Abert Rim rise abruptly from sage-covered basins.

Barrier and Bonanza

Yet for all its mountainous terrain, Oregon's ranges are really not that high. Mt. Hood, Oregon's loftiest summit at 11,235', would not even rate among the top 100 highest mountains in states like Colorado or California, and of the elevational high points in each of the 11 western states, Hood ranks last. In the entire state there are only five mountains over 10,000': Hood, Jefferson, North, Middle and South Sisters. But elevation alone is not necessarily a good yardstick with which to judge the character of mountains; more important is the amount of relief between the summit and the mountain's base. Hood, for example, rises dramatically from a base only 4,000' above sea level, while many mountains— say the 14,000' peaks of Colorado— rise from already high valleys that may be in excess of 10,000', giving them much lower relief.

While not possessing superlatives such as the highest or most rugged mountains in the West, Oregon's ranges may well be some of the most beautiful and as a landform they have influenced the state's past and future as much as any physical feature in the state.

The first mountains in Oregon seen by the European were those along the coast. Explorers bent on discovering the fabled Northwest Passage hurried by the unpromising shoreline that offered no harbors or possible sea passage through the mountainous terrain. These explorers were responsible for naming many features that they saw, even though many never set foot on the land which would become Oregon. Mt. Hood, for example, was named in 1792 for Lord Hood of England by Lieutenant Robert Broughton, who sailed up the northwest coast with Captain Vancouver. While Vancouver and other explorers failed to find a water route across the continent, they did discover a land rich in fur-bearing animals— the sea otter in particular.

By the late 1700s both American and British trading companies were trading in a three-part route. Sea otter pelts obtained from Pacific Coast Indians were taken to China and exchanged for tea and other goods from the Orient, which were traded in home ports on the east coast and in Europe. The typical trading venture lasted five years from the time a ship left its home port to the time of its return and the entire affair was fraught with many dangers including shipwreck, piracy, Indian attacks, and disease.

In 1805 Lewis and Clark reached the Pacific Coast, proving that a land route to the fur-rich west coast was feasible. The explorers also noted the abundance of beaver, which would soon replace sea otter pelts as the major object of trade. It was not long before land-based traders hoping to reduce the risks and time spent in trading ventures were crossing the continent to join the west coast fur trade. In 1811 a trading party financed by John Jacob Astor crossed the Rockies and established a post named Fort Astoria on the Columbia River. The enterprise failed, and in 1813 the fort was sold to the Northwest Fur Company, a Canadian rival of the Hudson's Bay Company. The two fur companies were merged in 1821, and by 1824 the Hudson's Bay Company had built Fort Vancouver on the Columbia River just opposite the site of today's Portland. Hudson's Bay Company employees such as Peter Skene Ogden and John Work were among the first Europeans to explore the hinterlands of what would become the state of Oregon. In addition, Americans like the fur trapper Jedediah Smith, whose party in 1828 became the first to come overland from California to Oregon, began to become acquainted with the region.

As part of a self-sufficiency program, Fort Vancouver built the first sawmill in the Pacific Northwest and also began a large farming operation. In a few years the fort was producing so much surplus lumber and agricultural products that it began to supply other posts as far away as Alaska.

Fort Vancouver's successful farming and lumber enterprises spurred the interest of land-hungry American settlers in the Midwest, who had heard about the rich soils and mild climate of the Oregon country from the many traders and trappers who had traveled through the region. By the 1840s increasing numbers of Americans began to move west over the Oregon Trail, to settle in the Willamette Valley. The influx of American settlers helped to solidify American claims to the Columbia Basin and in 1846 a treaty was signed between the United States and Great Britain, establishing the boundary of the American-controlled Oregon territory at 49 degrees north latitude. This subsequently became the U.S.-Canada border.

Today, nearly 70 percent of Oregon's 2,675,800 residents still make their home in the Willamette Valley. Half of the state's residents— 1.3 million people— live in the Portland area and most of the state's other urban residents live in other Willamette Valley communities including Salem,

Eugene, Corvallis and Albany. Outside of the area there are only a few other population centers: the Coos Bay area on the Coast; Grants Pass and Medford in the upper valleys of the Umpqua and Rogue rivers; and east of the Cascades, where the population thins, Klamath Falls and Bend. In the extreme northeast corner the pockets of habitation include La Grande, Ontario and Baker. The location of all of these communities near or in mountain valleys reflects the early settlers' concern for wood as building material, water for domestic and transportation purposes, and arable land for farming.

Although the Willamette Valley may seem thickly settled, the state as a whole is lightly populated. The population density (28 people per square mile) is more similar to Colorado (31 people per square mile) and other Rocky

The mild climate of the fertile Willamette Valley lying between the Coast and Cascade ranges first attracted white settlement. Pictured here is a farm near Veneta west of Eugene. GEORGE WUERTHNER

Facing page: The Oregon Coast Range meets the sea near Ecola State Park. LARRY ULRICH

7

Logging

Oregon's forests have for half a century fueled the state's economy, and today provide one in three residents with a job. Yet the settlers considered the region's giant trees a liability. One early homesteader complained: "The forests are so heavy and so matted with brambles, as to require the arm of a Hercules to clear a farm of 100 acres in an ordinary lifetime; the mass of timber is so great that an attempt to subdue it by girdling would result in the production of another forest before the ground could be disencumbered of what was thus killed."

The first people to see Oregon's forest cover in a positive light were the sailors plying the waters of the Pacific Northwest during the late 1700s. The tall, straight trees were cut for ships' spars and masts. By 1827 the Hudson's Bay post at Fort Vancouver set up the first saw mill in the Pacific Northwest and was selling lumber to points as far away as Alaska and California. Nevertheless, big-time logging was late in coming to the region; in 1899 Oregon ranked 23rd in the production of timber and did not outstrip Washington until the 1950s, when it became first in the nation.

Ironically it was the discovery of gold that prompted the first development of the West's timber. When gold was found in1848 in California, there were only a handful of sawmills operating on the entire West Coast. The influx of people to the gold fields soon dried up all timber supplies and many a ship with Maine lumber rounded Cape Horn bound for San Francisco. All the while the greatest forests on earth were growing literally out the back door. The soaring demand for timber soon sparked a timber rush that rivalled the original gold rushes, but there were giant problems to surmount before logging could become the big business it is today.

First, the trees of the western forests grew to amazing proportions, much larger than the trees that loggers had previously encountered in Maine and in the lake states. These giants required new techniques and tools, such as the springboard— a plank inserted in a notch in the trunk served as a platform from which the logger could attack the massive tree. The 10'-long falling saw and specially-designed axes with longer handles, allowed woodsmen to reach into the center of the large trees. It often took two men a day or more to fell one tree and the giant coastal redwoods in southern Oregon often required a week or more of constant work to topple. Getting a tree to the mill was another Herculean task. At first, most logging was concentrated near rivers or bays where logs could be floated to mills. Fallen timber was cut into manageable sections of 10' to 20' lengths, then dragged by a team of oxen to the water for final transport to the mill.

In steeper terrain, loggers built wooden flumes and chutes, some up to 50 miles long, down which logs were floated (in flumes) or simply slid (in chutes). An adventurous logger would often take a hair-raising trip to town by jumping on to a log as it started its journey down the flume; some logs reached speeds of 90 miles per hour.

Many loggers used natural flumes— rivers— to reach the mills. Dams were often built on headwater streams to store water for the log drive. When the impoundment was filled to capacity the loggers opened the spill gate and the rush of water swept logs downstream. Although an expedient means of transporting logs, such artificial floods destroyed many salmon and trout streams with their erosive force.

In the 1880s steam engines began to replace flumes and

Above: Early-day loggers worked from planks called springboards to attack the trunks of giant Douglas firs. Right: Oregon's rivers were an easy means of transporting logs to the mills. OREGON HISTORICAL SOCIETY PHOTOS. *Facing page: Water flumes or dry chutes, like Pokegama chute shown here, speeded the process.* COLLIER STATE PARK

the ox teams as means of transporting timber to the mills. Railroads, not limited by water or slope, were constructed back into the hills and opened up many new areas to the lumberjacks. The railroads also allowed lumbermen to get their product to markets. Once the transcontinental railroads were completed, the first in 1869, Oregon timber began to flow back east.

After World War II the final improvement in log transport came with the widespread use of the log truck, but this required the construction of thousands of miles of roads. There are now 87,598 miles of roads—enough to circle the globe three and a half times—on Forest Service lands in the 19 forests in the Pacific Northwest Region, which include 13 forests in Oregon and six in Washington. Besides Forest Service roads, there also are thousands of miles of logging roads on BLM, state and private timberlands. No one really knows what their aggregate impacts are on other resources such as wildlife and water quality.

Mountain states than to either of its West Coast neighbors. There are even portions of Oregon, such as the counties of the southeast corner, with less than one person per square mile—equaling the population density of Alaska!

Mountains Mean Trees

Besides influencing settlement, Oregon's mountains played an important role in its economic activity. The highlands wrench precipitation from the passing storm fronts and feed world-renowned forests of Douglas fir, Sitka spruce, ponderosa pine and hemlock that cover

Mountain hemlocks cling to Dutchman's Peak in the Siskiyou Mountains. GEORGE WUERTHNER

9

Agriculture and tourism rank behind the timber industry in the Oregon economy. This wheatfield is near Milton-Freewater on the edge of the Blue Mountains.

Facing page: Delicate branching of vine maple in the Drift Creek Wilderness of Oregon's Coast Range. The state's 36 designated wilderness areas provide glimpses of primeval beauty. GEORGE WUERTHNER PHOTOS

nearly half of Oregon and make it the most heavily forested state in the nation. This in turn has fueled the forest products industry that dominates the state's finances; one-third of the economy is directly or indirectly dependent on the extraction and milling of wood. The wood products industry generated $4.6 billon for the state in 1985.

Behind the timber industry are agriculture and tourism, the second and third ranking industries, each contributing more than a billon dollars to the state's economy per year. Even these activities are dependent on the mountains. For example, during the often dry Oregon summer much of the agricultural output relies upon irrigation water derived from mountain sources.

It is easy to see the connection between tourism and the mountains, to which people flock from around the world to fish, hunt, camp, swim, hike or simply view the outstanding natural environment. This industry is sustained by the vast public land holdings within Oregon. Only 30,625,000 acres—approximately half the state—are privately held. The rest is under some kind of federal management: 15.5 million acres administered by the U.S. Forest Service in 13 national forests and 16.5 million acres controlled by the Bureau of Land Management (BLM). There is just one national park, Crater Lake, but Oregon's conservation groups propose several more. These would include Steens Mountain; the entire Cascade Range in a Cascades Volcanoes Park; and a Siskiyou National Park in southwest Oregon that would encompass all of the western portion of these mountains from the Rogue River south to the California border. Oregon Dunes and Hells Canyon, two national recreation areas, highlight places of outstanding beauty and recent legislation created a Columbia Gorge National Scenic Area. On federal lands there are currently 36 designated wilderness areas totalling 2,097,193 acres, slightly smaller than the 2.2-million-acre Yellowstone National Park. Besides its federal lands Oregon has a well developed state park system, visited by more than 35 million in 1984. Tourism supports 61,000 jobs and is rapidly becoming one of the state's biggest employers, especially as other industries such as wood products continue their decline.

Mining has not played the significant role in the state's economy that it has in other western states. Most of Oregon's mountains are composed of volcanic basalts—rocks that typically harbor few valuable minerals. Except for portions of the Siskiyou and Blue mountains, where there were short-lived gold rushes, little mining occurred in Oregon's mountains and today the state's mineral industry produces less than $1.1 million worth of raw materials a year.

Finding employment is probably one of the more difficult aspects of living in Oregon, but for the fortunate employed, the rewards of living in the state are high. The state's generally acknowledged high quality of life stems primarily from its beautiful and relatively uncrowded natural environment. One can climb a glacier-clad peak, ski some of the best slopes on the West Coast, raft a whitewater river, or catch salmon out of a coastal bay all within a few hours of the major urban areas. And what Portland resident—frazzled by rush hour traffic or big city bustle—has not gotten a psychological boost from seeing Mt. Hood presiding over the city? Mountains set the stage upon which Oregon's human affairs have been conducted and their influence goes well beyond geographical statistics.

CHAPTER 2

Geology

Above: Basalt, seen here near the Clackamas River, is a rock of volcanic origins that covers much of Oregon. STEVE TERRILL

Right: Erosion-resistant basalt formation, which was once a conduit feeding an ancient volcano, remains as a line of sea stacks at Seal Rock State Park. GEORGE WUERTHNER

Viewed from the proper perspective, say from miles above the earth, it becomes obvious that mountains do not appear randomly over the globe, but rather are arranged in distinctive belts. Oregon, for example, has a line of coastal mountains parallel to the volcanic peaks of the Cascades, separated by the Willamette Valley. Beyond the Cascades are other mountain areas such as the Basin and Range region where uplifted ridges are arranged in a northwest-southeast direction. Geologists believe the theory of plate tectonics explains the ordering of these mountains, and even allows us to make some predictions about the future.

Mountain Geology: A Short Course

According to tectonic theory, the earth's crust is broken into a dozen or more pieces called plates, which float on the denser rocks of the earth's interior. These interior rocks are under such high pressure and heat that they become somewhat plastic and flow very slowly under the earth's crust, carrying with them the crustal plates much as northern rivers carry pans of ice after breaking up in the spring.

Like the river ice, pieces of these crustal plates collide and grind past each other while in other areas the plates are pulled apart. Into the gap created by spreading plates, melted basalt magma from the earth's interior rises and fills the opening. Plate spreading typically occurs in ocean basins and the new rock material solidifies to create new oceanic floor. Ocean seafloors, therefore, consist of layer upon layer of basalt flows similar in appearance to the massive basalt flows that cover much of eastern Oregon and the so-called scablands of eastern Washington.

At the same time that ocean floors are spreading apart and adding new rock material to their trailing edges, the advancing edges frequently collide with other plates. Some crustal material buckles up as mountains while other pieces are driven deep into the earth where they eventually become part of the earth's interior. Continental plates are made of lighter rock material than oceanic plates and hence float over the denser rock of the ocean floors.

Because of the migration and collision of continental and oceanic plates, the location and shape of the earth's land masses and oceans always is changing. For example, about 200 million years ago, during the time of the dinosaurs, the North American continent began to separate from part of a much larger plate that included the present continents of Europe and Africa. As the

developing North American plate began to drift westward, the Atlantic Ocean opened in its wake.

Approximately 150 million years ago the land mass that today is the state of Oregon did not exist. The west coast of North America ran in a line from approximately the present northeast corner of the state, by the Blue and Wallowa Mountains near the border of Idaho, in a southwest direction to what is now the Siskiyou (or Klamath) Mountains. West of this land mass was a broad, shallow continental shelf where muds and sands eroded from the mainland were deposited.

Along this collision line between North America and the Pacific plate, the ocean floor was being pushed under the advancing western edge of the North American continent. Coastal mountain ranges similar to those we see today along Oregon's north coast were created as the lighter continental rock was scraped off and piled up by the descending ocean floor. It must be remembered that

During the Ice Ages, so much of earth's water was captured as glacial ice that oceans were 300' lower than today. Rivers flowing into the sea cut deep canyons at their mouths, which were subsequently flooded after the glaciers melted. These "drowned" rivers form many of the tidal estuaries like Nestucca Bay north of Lincoln City.
GEORGE WUERTHNER

Shrinkage when molten rock cools creates multi-sided basalt pillars.

At right: South Sister has the typical cone shape of a stratovolcano, formed by alternating layers of lava flows and broken rock.
GEORGE WUERTHNER PHOTOS

coastal mountains do not always build up high enough to rise above sea level and may remain submerged or only partially exposed as offshore islands. Remnants of these former coastal mountains can be seen today in the rocks of the Siskiyou, Blue and Wallowa mountains which at that time were coastal mountains bordering the leading edge of the North American continental plate.

As the continental plate moved westward, the edge of the sinking seafloor migrated with it. New coastal mountains were created in central Oregon as the shoreline shifted to the west, but most of these newer mountains were subsequently buried under younger volcanic rocks that today cover much of central Oregon.

Inland and parallel to coastal mountains we usually find volcanoes. As oceanic rocks are driven deep into the earth under the advancing continental plate, they melt and create a source of molten basalt that subsequently rises toward the earth's surface along fractures in the crust. Melting and mixing with adjacent, lighter crustal sediments that make up the continental rock, the resulting amalgamation has a chemical composition different from pure basalt, usually much higher in silica. Silica is a mineral familiar to most people as the quartz sand that covers many beaches. This new rock material can either cool slowly in place, forming granite, or it can breach the surface as a volcanic eruption to form a green, brown or gray rock geologists call andesite.

Volcanoes

About 40 million years ago, a line of volcanoes ran north from the California border to the approximate location of today's Eugene, then curved eastward through the Ochoco Mountains beyond Redmond. Then some 35 million years ago there was a shift in the location of sea-floor sinking as the new line developed parallel to the present coastline of the state. This quieted volcanic activity for a while, until a new piece of the seafloor basin was driven deep enough into the mantle to melt and subsequently form a line of volcanoes that created the rocks we now see in the old Cascades. These volcanoes erupted on and off for some 10 million years.

Approximately 20 million years ago the volcanoes in the western Cascades grew silent while in central and eastern Oregon basalt began to erupt and flood the landscape, covering all of the state east of the Cascades and leaving only the highest parts of today's Blue and Wallowa mountains above the molten rock deluge. Eventu-

ally the central and eastern basalt flows ceased and new Cascade volcanoes became active.

The seafloor is still diving under the North American plate about 50 miles off the present coast of Oregon and is providing the magma source for today's High Cascades such as Mounts Hood, Jefferson and McLoughlin. While the North American plate sustains its westward movement we can expect continued volcanic activity into the near future.

Although the North American plate has been drifting in a general westerly direction, the western part of Oregon (but not the eastern) has been rifted slowly toward the north. The Basin and Range mountains in Oregon marking this line of structural stress are arranged along the Brothers fault zone. This area of fractured crust runs in a line from the southeast corner of the state by McDermitt, Nevada, northwest through the Bend area, runs under the Cascades and surfaces again in the Willamette Valley.

The Ice Ages

For the last 10 million years or so the state of Oregon has held its present general shape and outline, but during its entire geological history the climate was constantly shifting in response to world-wide climatic fluctuations as well as to the northward shift in latitude as the entire plate moved away from its original location that

Volcanoes

Geologists usually divide volcanoes into three types, which vary not only in physical appearance, but also in the chemical composition of their lavas. Basalt, the basic volcanic rock that comprises most of the ocean floors and also makes up a considerable amount of Oregon's lava plateaus, is a dense, fine-grained rock that usually contains about 50 percent silica. Basalt usually forms where portions of the oceanic crust melt between spreading ocean plates. Most basalt erupts under the surface of the sea, but occasionally it flows out on continents creating large plateaus such as those in eastern Oregon, Washington and parts of western Idaho.

Basalt eruptions typically produce volcanoes with gently-sloping sides that cover a broad surface area. These volcanoes usually have the gently domed appearance of a warrior's convex shield and are thus called shield volcanoes by geologists. The Hawaiian Islands are typical examples. Mt. Belknap in the Cascades by McKenzie Pass exemplifies the shield volcano landscape with a low surface profile, and black, broken rock that makes for rather monotonous scenery.

If by chance molten rock mixes with continental rocks such as granite or sedimentary rocks like sandstone, its silica content increases to between 54 and 60 percent to form a light gray, brown, or green rock called andesite. Andesite gets its name from the Andes Mountains in South America, which are composed primarily of these volcanic rocks. Because andesite is more viscous than basalt, it doesn't flow as quickly or as far from its crater and thus tends to build up steep-sloped cones that we usually associate with volcanoes. The Three Sisters, Mt. McLoughlin and Mt. Hood are examples of the andesite volcanoes that geologists term stratovolcanoes, because they consist of alternating layers of fluid lava flows and broken rock.

The third major rock type found in volcanic rocks is rhyolite. Its silica content is the highest of all, exceeding 64 percent, and it is the most viscous of volcanic rocks—something like modelling clay in consistency. It barely flows at all, taking on the appearance of a glacier whereas fluid basalts might look more like a river. The obsidian flows in Newberry Crater and on the south side of South Sister above Green Lake are two examples of rhyolitic rock that exhibit a glacier-like appearance. Because of rhyolite's viscosity it sometimes blocks the crater's vent. If water happens to soak into the hot, molten rock, incredible quantities of steam are produced and the usual culmination is an explosive eruption that empties the magma chamber something like a geyser spouting. Once emptied, the mountain often collapses into itself, as occurred 6,600 years ago to Mt. Mazama in the southern Cascades. Mazama's crater subsequently filled with water and created a future national park— Crater Lake.

After an eruption, accumulations of molten rock often plug the conduit permanently and further eruptions from the main vent are unlikely, although basalt cinder cones surrounding the main crater often erupt. Cinder cones, as their name implies, are composed of broken bits of rock blown out during an eruption. This material is called pyroclastic, which means "fire broken" in Greek. After bits of rock or cinders, are blown out, there is usually an accompanying lava flow or two. Once it completes its eruption, a cinder cone does not erupt again. Lava Butte and Pilot Butte by Bend are both examples of Oregon cinder cones.

Shield Volcano   Stratovolcano   Cinder Cone

Photos, left to right: Round basalt formation in Grande Ronde river canyon near Troy. Andesite flow along the rim of Crater Lake. Obsidian, sometimes called volcanic glass, at Newberry Crater.
GEORGE WUERTHNER PHOTOS

Clockwise from above: Dirt and rock embedded in a glacier will remain as a jumbled pile of material called a moraine when the ice melts. Rocks embedded in the bottom of a glacier will act like sandpaper to smooth bedrock; boulders left behind are called erratics.
Dirt-streaked surface of Carver Glacier on South Sister and horseshoe-shaped moraines. Small lakes called kettle ponds were formed when chunks of ice melted under their coverings of moraine debris.
A hiker examines a crevasse of the Lewis Glacier on South Sister.
GEORGE WUERTHNER PHOTOS

was closer to the equator. In addition to these long-term modifications local climatic permutations would have resulted from the rise of mountain ranges or the disappearance of seas. The most recent of these major climatic changes occurred within the last 3 million years and its effects on the mountains of the state are still plainly visable. During this time the overall temperature of the earth dropped several degrees and in the northern hemisphere the climate became wetter and cloudier. This period is known as the Ice Age.

While the large ice sheets that blanketed much of the northern half of the continent did not reach Oregon, glacial ice did mantle all the high peaks and uplands in the Cascades, as well as the higher regions of the Wallow-as, Elkhorns, Strawberrys, Greenhorns, and Steens

Mountains. Very small glaciers also formed on the Siskiyous, Gearhart Mountain and other isolated peaks.

Glacial ice forms whenever more snow accumulates than can melt for a number of succeeding years. This snow compacts, and like a glob of cold honey, slowly oozes downslope. Many geologists have likened a glacier to a slowly moving river and the analogy is appropriate in many ways, for like a river the ice breaks into waves whenever it flows over obstacles in the bedrock beneath it. The resultant cracks are called crevasses.

Rocks and gravel beneath and alongside the glacier are frozen into the ice and carried downslope as if on a giant conveyor belt. Eventually the point is reached where the ice melts as fast as it is replenished from above and the rocks and gravel pushed by the glacier and embedded in it are deposited in piles of unsorted material called a moraine. The farthest advance of a glacier often is marked by a horseshoe-shaped mound called the terminal moraine. In some cases the terminal moraine acts like a huge earthen dam and impounds the water from melting glaciers and normal run-off to form a lake. Wallowa Lake near Joseph, Oregon is an excellent example of a moraine–dammed lake.

Besides creating lakes and leaving piles of moraine littered over the landscape, glaciers also steepen the sides and flatten the bottoms of canyons as they grind their way downslope.

The catchment basins beneath the peaks and ridges where glaciers form usually take on a bowl-like appearance, as if they had been carved out by a giant ice-cream scoop. These natural amphitheaters are called cirques (rhymes with Turks). Where two cirque glaciers occupy and grind away at opposing sides of a ridge, they may create a knife-edge spine called an arete.

In addition to these large geomorphic features, glaciers also leave smaller markings upon the land. Rock embed ded in the bottom of the ice acts like sandpaper to grind, smooth and polish bedrock the glacier overrides. In many areas, the bedrock may be worn flat and many parallel scratches called striation lines are often visible. The conservationist John Muir referred to such striations as the "tracks" of glaciers, for like animal tracks they leave a record of past glacial movement.

The Ice Ages also left their mark in mountain ranges where little or no glacial ice formed. As difficult as it may be for someone who lives along Oregon's rain-drenched coast to imagine, it was even cloudier and rainier during the Ice Ages than at present. Because of the greater precipitation that accompanied the glacial period, down-cutting of river canyons was extremely rapid. The often rugged terrain of Oregon's Coast Range is due, in part, to this increased erosion.

In addition, the higher run-off filled the now predominantly dry basins of southeast Oregon. Summer, Abert, Harney, Malheur, Goose, Klamath and the Warner Lakes are remnants of much larger lakes that once filled these basins. The Christmas Lake, Catlow and Alvord valleys also once held lakes and though they now are dry, sage-covered expanses, one can still see the old shorelines, beaches and wave-cut terraces along the edges of hills and slopes. An abundance of arrowheads along these

terraces indicates that these lakes were popular hunting areas for the Indians.

Run-off from glacial rivers is typically milky white and dirty—full of pulverized rock sediments called glacial flour. When this glacial sediment is deposited on a riverbank and dries, it is easily carried on the wind as a light powdery dust called loess. The glaciers that once covered northern Idaho and Montana as well as the Cascades must have been large indeed, for they left a legacy of wind-blown dust deposits that now form the deep, productive soils of the wheat-growing Palouse region of eastern Washington and Oregon.

Even the incredible volume of dust required for loess deposition to depths of 20' or more in northeastern Oregon pales in comparison to the catastrophic impact

Glaciers typically steepen valley walls and smooth valley bottoms to create U-shaped canyons like the Kiger Gorge on Steens Mountain.
GEORGE WUERTHNER

of the immense floods that swept across eastern Washington and down the Columbia River during the height of the Ice Age. These floods originated in western Montana where giant lobes of glacial ice blocked the Clark Fork River, creating a thousand-foot-deep lake, which flooded most of the valleys in that region. These ice dams periodically ruptured and released surges of water estimated to equal ten times the combined flow of all the world's rivers! The raging wall of water raced across the land, scouring everything down to bedrock. Giant icebergs were rafted all the way to the Willamette Valley and left stranded on hillsides when the water subsided. These chunks of ice eventually melted and left behind piles of boulders and gravel that the glaciers had plucked from the peaks of western Montana.

Man on the Land

The first European settlers in Oregon came for the furs and later to till the soil, probably little concerned about geology or scenery. Nevertheless, after the discovery of gold in California in 1848, adventurers began to pay

attention to the state's rocks. Gold was found in 1852 on Jackson Creek near present-day Jacksonville, in southern Oregon's Siskiyou Mountains, and the discovery prompted a mass migration to the state's largely unpopulated regions. Jackson County soon boasted the largest population in Oregon. New discoveries followed in the Illinois River valley and elsewhere in the Rogue River drainage.

Although by 1860 western Oregon rapidly was becoming settled, eastern Oregon was virtually unexplored and had few residents except scattered groups of Indians who lived in the better hunting and foraging areas. Up until this time all gold strikes had been made in western Oregon, but in 1861 a prospecting party found gold on Griffen Creek on the Powder River near today's Baker. Within a year the town of Auburn, built near the discovery, could claim 5,000 residents. For a short time it was Oregon's largest community. Other strikes in eastern Oregon followed in rapid succession. Canyon City in the John Day Valley was discovered by prospectors bound for the Auburn mines and soon surpassed in value all

other gold placer diggings in the state. Placer gold was found in the Elkhorns, Wallowas, and the Greenhorns.

In one way or another all of Oregon's basic industries are tied to the state's geological past. The tourist industry relies on the spectacular scenery resulting from internal struggles between continental plates. The rich agricultural soils were created from glacial dust or rocks of volcanic origins. Even the mild, wet climate that helps to nurture the state's timber wealth can be traced to the region's geologic history, for without the climatic barrier created by the High Cascades, most of the annual precipitation that currently falls on the densely forested west slope might pass on to the east. Oregon's present can certainly be linked to its geologic past and in its geology lies its future as well.

Above: Volcanic ash of ancient eruptions formed the multicolored layers seen here at the John Day Fossil Beds.
Left: Obsidian flow near Paulina and East Lakes in Newberry Crater.

Facing page, top: The low grassy hill at the mouth of the canyon is a glacial moraine that has impounded water, creating Wallowa Lake in the Wallowa Mountains near the town of Joseph.
Bottom: Running water, particularly river current, has great erosive force— cutting channels through hard rock as it has through this gorge along the Breitenbush River in the Cascades.
GEORGE WUERTHNER PHOTOS

19

CHAPTER 3

Weather

Above: If you hike in western Oregon, you hike in the rain—more than 100" of precipitation falls annually in many areas.
Right: Oregon lies at the same latitude as Minnesota and southern Maine, yet enjoys an extremely mild climate as a result of the moderating effect of the Pacific Ocean. Seen at right, Heceta Head lighthouse.
GEORGE WUERTHNER PHOTOS

Oregon's climate is influenced by its proximity to the Pacific Ocean. Air masses typically move from the sea along the western portion of the state and travel eastward bringing mild temperatures and abundant precipitation. A moisture-laden air mass coming into Oregon off the Pacific first encounters the coastal mountains, which force the air masses to rise and cool. The ability of air to hold water is dependent upon its temperature. The colder the air the less moisture it can hold. Tropical areas feel uncomfortably humid, while polar regions are often referred to as cold deserts. In crossing the mountains air masses lose their ability to hold moisture and consequently Oregon's coastal mountains are deluged with their legendary heavy rainfall. For example, the little town of Valsetz in the Coast Range northwest of Corvallis receives an average of 126" of precipitation a year!

Once an air mass has passed over a mountain barrier it sinks and warms, increasing its ability to hold moisture. Precipitation tapers off or ceases altogether. Such leeward sinking air masses may even absorb moisture from the land, creating an environment more arid than mere rainfall statistics might indicate. Dry valleys to the lee of the mountains are frequently said to lie in the "rain shadow" of the range. Eugene in the Willamette Valley receives 42" of annual precipitation, while Bend to the east on the other side of the cloud-wrenching Cascades, has an annual average of only 12". An ad for recreation property in the Eugene newspaper reads: "Why sit in the rain when you can live in the sun? Five acre cabin site located in pines near Bend." The ad was obviously appealing to Willamette Valley residents who must endure long rainy winters while the sun shines unstintingly on Bend and other communities east of the Cascades.

The Moderate West, The East of Extremes

But precipitation is not the only factor influenced by mountains and their proximity to water bodies. The ocean's ability to hold heat moderates the temperatures experienced by coastal communities. Freezing temperatures are unusual in winter, while summers remain cool. For example, the average January high and low temperature in coastal Newport are 50 and 37 and in July 64 and 50 degrees, while at Salem—just inland across the Coast Range—the January temperatures are colder, with average high and low at 46 and 33 degrees and in July much warmer when the average high is 82 and the low, 50 degrees. The Coast Range acts as a barrier, insulating the Willamette Valley from the moderating influences of the nearby ocean. Nevertheless, maritime influences are not

totally blocked and the Willamette Valley is relatively mild and rainy for its latitude.

East of the Cascades it is another story. The Cascades are high enough to be a major hurdle to Pacific air masses from the west and also to block cold continental fronts from the east. The result is much greater temperature range for the communities east of the mountains. For example, Madras is less than a hundred miles from Salem, but on the eastern side of the Cascades, the average high and low in January are 42 and 22 degrees, while the July average high and low are 87 and 46, much more extreme than either the Willamette Valley or the coast.

Brookings is sandwiched between the Pacific Ocean and the Siskiyou Mountains and has one of the most moderate climates in the state, as well as a correspondingly high annual precipitation. Burns, in east central Oregon, is at the other extreme, with some of the coldest winter temperatures and very warm summers. The hottest temperatures in the state are recorded for areas along the Columbia and Snake rivers in the eastern portions of the state— the July average high for Ontario on the Snake River is 96 degrees.

Because of the modifying influence of the Pacific Ocean and the barrier to cold-air flow created by the Cascades, Portland has one of the more equable climates of major U.S. cities. Lying in the rain shadow of the Coast Range,

Representative Oregon Weather Stations

Station	Average Precip. (inches/yr.)	January Avg. Temp. High-Low	July Avg. Temp. High-Low
Astoria	69.59	47-35	68-52
Portland	37.38	44-34	80-56
Brookings	76.22	54-41	66-51
Medford	19.84	45-30	91-54
Bend	11.53	41-21	82-44
Madras	9.61	42-22	87-46
Baker	11.89	35-18	86-50
Burns	10.31	37-18	84-54
Ontario	9.60	37-21	96-57
Salem	40.35	46-33	82-50
Enterprise	13.08	34-14	83-43

Top: Winters are long and summers brief in most mountains because of the elevation. Here ice on a lake in the Eagle Cap Wilderness breaks up in July.

Bottom: The small ranch community of Andrews, lying in the rainshadow of Steens Mountain in eastern Oregon, is the driest reporting weather station in the state, with average annual precipitation of only 7". GEORGE WUERTHNER PHOTOS

Portland's annual average precipitation is only 37" as compared to New York City with 44", Miami, Florida with 57.5" and Mobile, Alabama with 64.6". Even its infamous reputation for cloudy skies is really undeserved. Portland has sunny skies an average of 47 percent of the time, which compares favorably with such eastern cities as Cleveland, Ohio (49 percent), Burlington, Vermont (49 percent), and Pittsburgh, Pennsylvania (47 percent sunshine).

The typically rainy winters in Oregon are due to the southward migration of North Pacific lows bringing mild, moist air masses to the North American coast. In summer, the low retreats toward Alaska and allows a high pressure system to cover the state. The stable high brings sunny, dry weather. Monthly extremes for Salem, which receives 7" in January and only .35" in July, exemplify these trends. Although the total amount of precipitation varies from station to station in the state, all show the same pronounced summer drought and winter moisture pattern.

The abundance of winter storms means that most of the annual precipitation falls as snow, particularly in the higher elevations. As Pacific air moves up and over such barriers as the Cascades, most of the moisture falls out as heavy, wet snow on the western slopes, but on the frequently colder east side of the divide, the moisture is precipitated out as light and dry snow— the stuff that ski buffs call "powder." Bachelor Butte Ski Area, east of the Cascades divide by Bend, and Anthony Lakes Ski Area near Baker are renowned for their powder snow.

Next Summer's Water

The slow melting of the winter's mountain snowpack provides the steady summer supply of water for irrigation, recreation, fisheries, and domestic purposes. In parts of the state such as the western portion of the Siskiyous where the elevations are rather low, many streams and rivers suffer a drastic seasonal fluctuation in water flow between the highs of the rainy winter and the lows of late summer.

Although rare, in some winters a high pressure system invades the state bringing bitterly cold weather and clear skies, even west of the Cascades. Portland's record low of minus 7 was set during one of these infrequent blasts of cold Arctic air. If these high pressure zones persist, the loss of snowfall and subsequent water storage in the mountains can seriously affect water users the following summer.

While the most precipitation comes in winter storms, all of Oregon experiences some summer rainfall, and in many places this comes as thunderstorms. In the summer, heating of air near the earth's surface causes it to rise rapidly. Any moisture in the air can contribute to puffy cumulus clouds that can eventually build into thunderheads. This phenomenon is particularly prevalent over mountains since hot air from the valleys expands and forces it to rise and cool. As the warm air rises, cool air above it is displaced and sinks to generate the gusty winds we often associate with the approach of thunderstorms.

When the air has cooled sufficiently water droplets form and rain begins to fall. The rain can turn to hail if the droplets encounter freezing temperatures. Individual hail pellets increase in size if swept upward by strong air drafts that typify mountain areas. A new layer of ice is added on each successive ascent. Eventually the weight of the ice is so great that the hail pours out of the sky to pound whatever and whoever is unfortunate enough to be in its path.

Mountains are windy places. In the evening, cold air surrounding the upper heights of a mountain begins to sink to fill the valleys and basins, while the ridges are comparatively warmer. (Good gardeners know to plant on benches rather than on stream bottoms, which are the first areas to frost.) This cold air drainage also affects mountain vegetation, with many cirque basins having trees susceptible to frost damage, particularly as seedlings, flourishing only on ridges while the valley floors are covered with meadows.

As the air warms it rises, creating an upslope breeze during the day. The afternoon is usually the breezy time of the day when heating and consequent rise of air are most pronounced. The flow of air tapers as the day cools, bringing the evening calm known well to fly fishermen who find this time of day perfect for their sport.

Like water rushing between two rocks, air moving through a pass or a canyon is squeezed into a smaller space, and accelerates to make the passage. In addition to these physical factors, high mountains also tend to intercept more high-level winds that seldom ruffle the valleys below them.

The movement of an air mass through a narrow gap also increases precipitation. The compression of moisture-laden air as it moves through a small opening wrings water from the clouds; hence narrow valleys receive more precipitation than wide-open valleys at the same eleva-

tion and general location. In addition, because such valleys are shadier they maintain a higher average humidity and in general appear wetter than their broader counterparts elsewhere. In summer, elk, bear and other animals seek shelter from the heat in dark, constricted canyons.

Mountains modify Oregon's weather. Because of them raincoats and umbrellas are standard gear in Eugene while east of the Cascades, in Bend, sunglasses and down coats are fashionable. Without mountains the diversity of landscapes and climates that most people take for granted would not exist.

Hundreds of miles from the moisture-producing ocean, and lying in the rainshadow of high peaks, the Alvord Desert below Steens Mountain is one of the driest places in Oregon.

Facing page: Air masses ascending mountains cool, and precipitation often results, feeding western Oregon's many rivers and lush forests. Oak Fork Clackamas River. GEORGE WUERTHNER PHOTOS

CHAPTER 4

Mountain Vegetation

Above: Western juniper and yellow rabbitbrush east of Bend.

Right: Old-growth Sitka spruce along Rock Creek in Oregon's Coast Range. GEORGE WUERTHNER PHOTOS

Forests define Oregon in people's minds as much as anything; they think of its reputation for giant trees, logging and mills. Oregon has no shortage of trees, although the entire state is certainly not cloaked with verdant growth, as anyone who has ever traveled through the southeast portion can testify. Yet, trees— big trees— do shape Oregon's self-image, and for good reason.

Nearly half the state is forested— a higher percentage than in any other western state. These woodlands support Oregon's forest products industry, but not all sections of the state rely upon the same species of trees for their mills. A mill in Bend processes ponderosa pine, while its counterpart along the coast might be sawing Sitka spruce and western hemlock.

Just why Sitka spruce should grow on the coast, while it is absent from the Cascades or why western larch is restricted to forests east of the Cascades, is explained by a host of environmental factors including precipitation, temperature, elevation, wind, soil, past geological and geographical history, and the impact of humans from ancient times to the present. These, acting in concert with each species' individual genetic make-up, determine just what will grow and where.

Two Forest Provinces

Oregon has two major forest belts separated by the Cascade Mountains. To the east are some of the most spectacular ponderosa pine forests in the world, which cover broad areas on the lower slopes of the Cascades and the various highlands of the Blue Mountains complex. Associated with these ponderosa forests are western larch, grand fir and lodgepole pine. Grasses like bluebunch wheatgrass and pinegrass or shrubs such as snowberry and bitterbrush cover the forest floor.

In the warmer, drier reaches of these eastern Oregon mountains and in the more arid Basin and Range province western juniper forms savanna-like stands amid big sagebrush and grasses. In the wetter vales and north-facing slopes of this very dry region one finds aspen, a species widely scattered over central and eastern Oregon, but nowhere as abundant as farther east in the Rockies. On some island-like ranges such as Hart Mountain and Steens Mountain, aspen forms the bulk of the limited tree cover.

From the Klamath Lake region and westward into the Siskiyou Mountains, there is a real mix of tree and plant types. From the south are trees typical of the California forests including black oak, golden chinquapin, knobcone pine, Jeffery pine, Shasta red fir and, along the coast, the most northern extension of redwood. From the north are the Cascade influences with subalpine fir and western red cedar, along with a host of endemic species including Brewers Spruce and Port Orford cedar. Understory plants include thimbleberry, snowbrush, bracken fern and Pacific dogwood.

On the west slope of the Cascades grow the towering forests of Douglas fir mixed with western hemlock, and higher up the slopes one finds noble fir and mountain hemlock. Beneath the shady canopy are sword fern, huckleberries, and deciduous trees like big leaf and vine maple.

The coastal forests consist of large stands of old-growth Sitka spruce, Douglas fir and western hemlock intermixed with smaller amounts of Port Orford and western red cedar. On well drained sandy coastal sites grows the lodgepole pine, while big leaf maple and red alder concentrate along watercourses. Understory plants include salmonberry, salal, fool's huckleberry, and evergreen huckleberry.

Trees require at least two months where daytime temperatures average higher than 50 degrees; areas above this temperature isotherm are either barren or covered

with alpine tundra. Since few of Oregon's mountains are exceptionally high, alpine areas are limited, with the best representation found in the Wallowa Mountains, and other isolated occurrences on Steens Mountain, and the higher Cascade peaks like Mt. Hood and the Three Sisters.

Frontier for Trees—Timberline

Although few alpine areas exist, many Oregon mountains reach or approach timberline— the limit to tree growth. Surprisingly, timberline is actually lower where the climate is wetter, even if average temperatures are

Clockwise from top left: Lodgepole pine grows along the coast and in the Cascades and Blues. Ponderosa pine forms nearly pure stands at low elevations east of the Cascades and throughout the Blues. Water-loving hardwoods like these red alder in the Rock Creek Wilderness in the Coast Range are usually restricted to moist sites. Noble fir is common in the Cascades and Siskiyous, but rare in the Coast Range, such as Mary's Peak here. GEORGE WUERTHNER PHOTOS

Top: Sub-alpine krummholz on Strawberry Mountain. Bottom: Drought-tolerant sagebrush and yellow-flowered buckwheat in Gearhart Mountain Wilderness. Right top: Vine maple along Clackamas River. Right bottom: lush ferns in the well-watered Cummin Creek Wilderness.
GEORGE WUERTHNER PHOTOS

not extreme. Thus timberline drops farther down the mountain on Mt. Hood than on Mt. McLoughlin, south of Crater Lake, where it is sunnier and drier.

Timberline varies in elevation on the same mountain. Southwest exposures receive the greatest amount of incoming solar radiation and are warmer than north and northeast slopes, which are shaded. As a result, where cold temperatures limit the growth of trees, timberline often is several hundred feet higher on south slopes than north.

Different tree species react differently to the stresses of timberline. For instance, near the top of Strawberry Peak in the Strawberry Mountains subalpine fir assumes a low, twisted form, while whitebark pine in the same location is a stout, though short, upright tree.

Cold air drainage also is a factor in determining timberline. Cold night air sinks into cirque basins and drops temperatures 15 to 20 degrees lower than on the ridges above. Cold air drainage also can influence tree distribution at lower elevations. East of the Cascades, among what would otherwise be continuous ponderosa pine forest, one finds extensive stands of lodgepole pine. Lodgepole is a frost-hardy species that occupies depressions where cold air collects, while the frost-sensitive ponderosa covers every knob and ridge that rises above these frost basins. At higher elevations it is common to find meadows in the bottoms of cold-air drainage basins, while trees are restricted to the surrounding ridges. In some areas, logging can change patterns of cold air drainage and effectively thwart reforestation efforts if a formerly forested basin becomes a trap for sinking, cold night air.

Wind also influences the distribution of trees and other plants. Winds can snap branches as well as grind plant surfaces with wind-blown dirt and sand. In addition, wind affects the deposition of snow, which can bury plants under a protective insulation. Trees or plants without snow cover must endure temperature extremes and often suffer from desiccation. Near timberline and along the coastal headlands, many of these trees take on a wind-sheared appearance, growing branches on the lee side of the trunk where snow can accumulate and give some protection to the bough. At extreme locations, the trees take on a stunted, crawling posture called krummholz, which in German means "twisted stick." But wind also helps plants disperse pollen and seeds.

Besides an upper timberline, many mountains also have a lower timberline where drought and heat limit tree

growth. In the eastern portion of the state lower timber-line is usually marked by ponderosa pine or western juniper. West of the Cascades in the valleys of the Rogue, Umpqua, and Willamette lower timberline is fringed by white oak, black oak, and Douglas fir— although even here one may find an occasional ponderosa pine. Before the arrival of the white man, Indians set fires to the grasslands both east and west of the Cascades and kept many of the lower valleys in a sub-climax grassland or savanna. With the advent of fire suppression, trees have now invaded many areas formerly excluded to them by frequent burns and lower timberline has crept down hillsides as a result.

Most mountains exhibit clearly marked zones by altitude that reflect changes in moisture and temperature. Coupled with these general trends are many local micro-climatic factors that affect the ultimate distribution of any species. Species requiring moist, cool conditions descend far down a mountain in shady canyons, while drought-tolerant species grow low on the mountain as well as near the summit on well drained, wind-blown sites where droughty conditions persist.

This zonation is readily visible when ascending the trans-Cascade passes south of Bend. If you climb from the grass and sage-covered high desert east of the Cascades you'll first encounter western juniper growing in open woodlands. As you ascend the fringes of the mountains you enter beautiful open ponderosa pine forest which may, with increasing altitude, intermix with white fir. In areas of cold drainage, the ubiquitous lodgepole pine may be found scattered among the ponderosa and white fir stands. At higher elevations the shasta red fir forests dominate to nearly timberline, where it is replaced by mountain hemlock and whitebark pine at the final limits to tree growth. The species mix will change from region to region, but the principle remains the same.

Plants of the High Desert

Forests, of course, are the lifeblood of the state, but to the east, beyond the Cascade crest and south of the Blue Mountains stretches an immense region too arid for trees and covered with grass and sage— what locals call the High Desert. In many places, due primarily to over-grazing coupled with fire suppression, the native bunch-grasses have been reduced and often replaced by shrubs such as sagebrush, or less desirable grasses like cheat-grass. It would be wrong to imply that sagebrush was never here, for old records and journals frequently men-tion sagebrush or "wormwood" as it was sometimes called; nevertheless these shrubs have increased in density in some areas as grazing has eliminated competing grasses.

Grasses are superbly adapted to this arid environment. The native species like bluebunch wheatgrass are called cool-season grasses because they do most of their growth in the spring, to take advantage of spring rains and soil moisture accumulated during the winter. When the region's characteristic summer drought arrives in late June or early July, the grass already has produced its seeds and gone into dormancy. Excess carbohydrates are withdrawn from its leaves and stored in the plant's roots. If autumn brings rainy weather, bluebunch and other cold-season grasses will again green up and photosynthesize until winter brings on dormancy. Grasses can thus avoid the seasons when growth is impossible.

Unlike a tree that has a large percentage of its biomass above ground, grasses usually have more below ground in an extensive root system that scours the soil for available moisture and also stores excess food produced by the leaves above. As a lush manicured lawn shows, grasses can survive periodic cropping, and this is the theory under which grazing management developed. When a grass is clipped, whether by a lawn mower or a cow, it immediately transfers food resources from its roots to the above-ground parts to assist in the construction of new leaves. Once the leaves are grown, the plant resumes its task of storing food and extending the root system necessary to survive in a world of periodic drought. If a plant is cropped too frequently, it may not die outright but is surely weakened, for instead of adding to the all-important root system, it must repeatedly regrow the above-ground leaves. If a drought ensues, it will be this plant that dies first, and therefore we must water our closely clipped lawns so frequently.

Most grazing animals— whether wild or domestic— eat selectively. Certain grasses or browse plants are favored because they are nutritious, tender, abundant, or simply taste good. For whatever reason, if given a choice an animal will eat some species before others. On range-lands these plants are known as decreasers in this selection process by grazers. Other plants, called increasers, are freed of competition from the decreasers, and will rush in to fill the void. If grazing pressure is extremely heavy, even these will disappear and virtually unpalatable species will come to dominate the site. Range managers call these invaders; most other people know them by a less scientific term— weeds.

Top: Arrowleaf balsamroot, a common spring flower in the drier parts of Oregon.
Bottom: Purple mountain saxifrage, an alpine species that grows in a tight cluster close to the ground to conserve heat and moisture.
GEORGE WUERTHNER PHOTOS

Fire Ecology

When the first white settlers arrived in Oregon they found much of the Willamette and other western valleys, like the upper Rogue, to be open grasslands with fringes of forest confined to river courses and rocky knolls. Early travelers frequently described the ponderosa pine forests east of the Cascades as having an open, park-like appearance. One explorer noted that these woodlands "were so open we could give our horses rein and let them wander at will."

These prairies and open low-elevation forests were maintained by wildfire—both lightning and human ignited—and burned at three- to 20-year intervals. Many of these blazes were set by Indians who used fires to clear brush, to confuse game when hunting or to signal other Indians. Near present-day Vale, trapper Peter Skene Ogden wrote on July 14, 1827: "The country on all sides is on fire, these are signals for Indians to assemble as they shortly will steer their course to Buffaloe." In 1834 Captain Bonneville wrote that the valleys of the Powder and Grande Ronde rivers were "wrapped in one vast conflagration." Such fires spread through the grassy understory, killing saplings but seldom harming the large, thick-barked old-growth trees.

Many western coniferous forests evolved with fire as a natural component of the environment and depend upon these blazes for regulation of competition, recycling of nutrients, and control of the frequency and magnitude of insect and forest pathogen outbreaks. The thick bark on mature ponderosa pine, sugar pine, western larch, and Douglas fir protect their inner cambium layers which supply new growth from all but the most intense heat. Many old forest giants bear fire scars. By comparing the age and frequency of these scars from many trees, forest researchers can construct the fire history of the region.

In addition to thick bark, these same species tend to self-prune so that the resulting bole is free of branches for many feet above the ground. Thus small understory fires are less likely to ignite the upper parts of the tree, or "crown out" as firefighters call it. The fires kill only the smaller saplings whose bark is not thick enough to protect the sensitive inner layers.

These small, periodic fires were beneficial in many ways. First, they eliminated fuel build-ups that would otherwise lead to a hotter fire—one more likely to crown out and kill the mature trees outright. And frequent blazes created natural fire-breaks, by making fuels too sparse to carry flames.

In addition, the periodic fire thinning meant the remaining trees had less competition and thus grew faster, were healthier and more resistant to insects and disease. It is no coincidence that outbreaks of pine beetle, spruce budworm and other forest pathogens have increased in

Ponderosa pine (above) requires periodic fires to eliminate competition from its own progeny and other species. Right: Forest fires, like this one along the John Day River, were once a common feature of natural ecological processes.
GEORGE WUERTHNER PHOTOS

severity and frequency since fire suppression began. By putting out fires we are actually making the forests less healthy and more prone to massive epidemic outbreaks. Not all forests burned on short intervals. In wetter areas such as the western Cascades or along the coast, fires were less frequent and fuel loading was higher. The resulting fires were often very hot and catastrophic. And so, even these forests evolved under a regime of periodic fires, although the time scale was stretched to intervals of several hundred years.

Most fires go out after burning just a few acres, but there are "fire years" when conditions of drought, wind and humidity are such that fires take off and burn thousands of acres. In the hundred years between 1811 and 1911, major fires burned an estimated 4 million acres in Oregon. Most of this acreage was burned in a few major fires including the Nestucca Fire of 1848 which burned 300,000 acres, the Siuslaw and Siletz Rivers Fires in 1849 which consumed 800,000 acres, the 1853 Yaquina Fire which burned 480,000 acres, and the 1868 Coos Bay Fire which overran 300,000 acres. The last major fire was the Tillamook Burn which was actually three different fires that burned 240,000 acres in 1933, 189,000 acres in 1939, and in 1945, 173,000 acres.

Since World War II and the advent of modern fire fighting technology, no fires have approached the magnitude of these historic conflagrations. Today an average of 5,000 acres burns each year on Oregon's national forests. For instance, in 1976 there were 918 fires on national forests in Oregon, consuming 1,475 acres. In 1977, 1,678 fires overran 11,997 acres, in 1978 1,220 fires burned 3,756 acres, and in 1985, 972 fires burned 4,754 acres. As of late 1986, complete records for the year were not available, but it was a particularly good year for fires, and an estimated 120,000 acres burned in the state. Compare these records with those from the previous century and it's easy to understand why fuels are building and disease and insect infestations are on the rise.

Obviously it would be impractical to let all fires burn uncontrolled as in the past, but fires can be monitored at much less cost than all-out suppression. Indeed, in many wilderness areas and areas with low productivity forests, monitoring is all that is required. Prescribed burns can be, and are, used by land managers to reduce fuel loads near towns, homes and other property, thus helping to reduce the potential for major, life–threatening conflagrations.

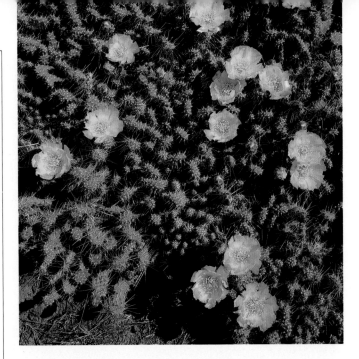

Cactuses, such as these in Morrow County, conserve water in an arid environment by eliminating leaves and relying on chlorophyll in their pads to produce food. STEVE TERRILL

In eastern Oregon the dominant native perennial grass is bluebunch wheatgrass— a decreaser. Because of overgrazing, bluebunch has dramatically declined over much of its range. In its place grows the less desirable increaser— Sandberg bluegrass, and in many places an annual invader— cheatgrass.

Cheatgrass, a species introduced from Europe, now dominates many low-elevation areas of eastern Oregon. In a wet spring a cloak of this grass mantles the land providing fair forage for livestock, but unlike native perennials it quickly loses its nutritional value after curing. In addition, cheatgrass is highly flammable and thousands of acres of cheatgrass range burn each year. This actually increases the dominance of the grass, because the annual cheatgrass will have shed its seeds prior to the fire season and many seeds will survive the flames to revegetate the area the following spring. Although nearly all grasses tolerate periodic wildfires, most cannot burn year after year without serious declines. Thus where cheatgrass is abundant, other more desirable grasses may disappear.

Oregon's mountain vegetation is more than the fuel for timber and grazing industries, for it provides the natural landscaping that gives the state its overwhelming beauty, serves to protect watersheds and is home to the state's wildlife populations.

CHAPTER 5

Wildlife

Above: Mountain chickadee, busy and fearless inhabitant of high coniferous forests. JAN WASSINK

Right: The bobcat feeds primarily on small rodents, rabbits and birds. DAN DAVIDSON

Oregon's mountains provide a variety of wildlife habitats, from the densely forested, lush Coast Range to the sagebrush-covered desert slopes of the Sheepshead and Trout Creek mountains. The high Cascade Range, because of its lack of low passes and its influence on climate, forms a major barrier between species adapted to the moist, forested areas west of the range and the drier, open country of eastern Oregon. Mountain beaver, brush rabbit, shrew-mole, dusty footed wood rat, and Townsend's vole are all mammals limited to areas west of the Cascades. East of the Cascades one finds species designed to exploit open, dry country like Ord's kangaroo rat, badger, sagebrush vole, white-tailed jackrabbit, yellow-bellied marmot, Nuttall's cottontail, pronghorn antelope and desert wood rat.

Some species live on both sides of the Cascades, but are separated into different sub-species. Thus to the east of the Cascades one finds the mule deer and Rocky Mountain elk while west of the range are the blacktail deer and Roosevelt elk. Where sub-species intermix on the crest of the Cascades, hybrids with features typical of both sub-species occur.

Species distributed in appropriate habitat over the entire state are bobcat, coyote, porcupine, mountain lion, beaver, mink and otter. In addition, more than 400 species of birds are recorded for Oregon. Many, with the exception of sea birds, can be found in the mountains and hills of the state. These species include the red-tailed hawk, kestrel, mourning dove, great horned owl, common flicker, black-capped chickadee, robin, western bluebird, western meadowlark, and red-winged blackbird. Nevertheless, drastically different climates and habitats found on either side of the Cascade Range restrict some bird species. The sage sparrow, sandhill crane, and bank swallow are found only east of the Cascades. Other species like the spotted owl may occasionally be found on the east slope of the range, but are far more numerous west of this major dividing line.

To the East: Antelope and Sage Grouse

Throughout eastern Oregon, the low-elevation landscapes are dominated by sagebrush, grasslands, and juniper-savanna. One of the largest native species of mammal found here is the pronghorn antelope. They once roamed over all of southeast Oregon and ranged north to The Dalles and even into the grassy, upper portions of the Rogue River valley. Today an estimated 10,000 to 15,000 antelope inhabit the southeast portion of the state. They can be found roaming on gentle slopes in many mountain ranges including Hart Mountain, the

Above: Although popularly associated with deserts and plains, the coyote is found throughout Oregon, even in the dense coniferous forests west of the Cascades. JAN WASSINK
Left top: Oregon's numerous rivers, particularly in the western part of the state, support river otters. JAN WASSINK
Left bottom: The shy mountain beaver lives in the lush coniferous forests west of the Cascades and is seldom seen by people. TOM AND PAT LEESON

have died trapped against a fence when the shelter they sought lay on the far side of the obstruction.

Another dweller of the arid spaces is Ord's kangaroo rat. While driving across eastern Oregon at night, I have often seen these small, light brown rodents hopping across the roads. This kangaroo rat will drink water if available, but can survive for months without a drink through several adaptations: an extremely efficient kidney which pulls all water from its feces before eliminating them from the body, and the ability to metabolize water from the seeds it eats. In addition, the Ord's kangaroo rat remains in its burrow with entrances blocked when humidity is low and comes out only at night when evaporative losses are lower.

Stalking the kangaroo rat, lizards, beetles and other denizens of the arid grass-sage mountains of eastern Oregon is an unusual killer— the northern grasshopper mouse. This carnivorous mouse shares many similarities with other social predators. Like a miniature coyote, the grasshopper mouse howls, emitting a long, high-pitched wail. And there are other peculiarities. Unlike most other mice species, the male grasshopper mouse helps raise its young, bringing food back to the burrow. The previous litter of non-breeding but mature young grasshopper mice will help the parents raise the next generation. Grasshopper mice also stake out large territories, which they defend vigorously against trespass.

Preying on these nighttime rodents is the great horned owl, the most widespread owl in Oregon. As with all owls, their hearing is extremely keen. An owl can track the movement of an animal in total darkness by comparing the micro-second delay in sound reaching one ear as opposed to the other. The owl's soft feathers produce almost no sound as it flies, enabling it to swoop silently down on prey.

One of the more interesting annual rites on the sagebrush mountains of eastern Oregon is the sage grouse lek display. In late February and early March male sage grouse gather at traditional courtship display areas, which usually are open flats surrounded by sagebrush. Generation after generation of grouse use the same traditional strutting grounds. One lek in Idaho is thought to have been in use for more than 90 years. Next to each lek there must be some dense shrub cover where birds can hide from predators; unfortunately these densely canopied sites are the kind range managers typically eliminate to create greater forage for livestock production. This is one reason sage grouse numbers have been declining over much of the West.

Top: Antelope inhabit the arid eastern Oregon mountain ranges.
GEORGE WUERTHNER
Bottom: The tiny pygmy owl is no bigger than a small grapefruit.
JAN WASSINK

Pueblo Mountains, Sheepshead Mountains and even the Blue Mountain complex north of Burns. Since these fleet-footed animals (I have clocked them at better than 45 miles per hour for short bursts) rely on their keen eyesight to spot predators, they avoid densely wooded areas and keep to the open country. Unlike deer and elk, both sexes of antelope have horns, though those of the male are typically larger and "pronged." Horns are shed annually and a new skin grows over the bony core each spring, which eventually manufactures a sheath made of much the same material as human fingernails and hair.

Since southeast Oregon, where the majority of Oregon's antelope are found, is also the coldest portion of the state, it might be surmised that pronghorn have adaptations for cold weather, and, indeed, their hides are extremely good insulation. The hairs are hollow and work on the same principle as the down coat, trapping dead air close to the body where it heats. In severely cold weather, however, this is not enough and the pronghorn seeks out shelter in the lee of sagebrush and other shrubs. Antelope will not readily jump fences like deer, and fencing on the rangelands of the West has often hindered their movements. In stormy weather entire herds

In Oregon, sage grouse once ranged north to the Columbia River from The Dalles to the Pendleton and south to Klamath Lake. Today their range is restricted to areas south of the Blue Mountain complex and east of Klamath Lake. Sage grouse rely almost entirely upon sagebrush for food and habitat. Range "improvement" programs like the 4.6-million-acre Vale Project, which replaced sagebrush with exotic grasses like crested wheatgrass, seriously deplete sage grouse populations even within their current natural range by eliminating the necessary sagebrush.

Although sage grouse tend to nest under the canopy of dense sagebrush stands, they prefer to be close to wet meadows where young chicks forage for insects and succulent plants during the first few weeks of life. Overgrazing removes riparian vegetation and thereby accelerates erosion and stream down-cutting, lowering the local water table. Eventually these abused wet meadows disappear and are replaced by sagebrush and other species better adapted to the altered conditions.

Heritage Lost, Heritage Found

Contrasting with the sage grouse's reliance on sagebrush, bighorn sheep depend on grasslands. Prior to the ravages of livestock grazing in eastern Oregon, native grasses like bluebunch wheatgrass and Idaho fescue supported numerous small populations of Rocky Mountain and California bighorn sheep. Wild sheep disappeared from most of their native ranges as disease introduced from domestic herds, a loss of habitat due to overgrazing by livestock, and market hunting all took their toll. In recent years, bighorn sheep have been reintroduced into many eastern Oregon mountains including Hart Mountain, Steens Mountain, and around the Wallowa Mountains.

Sheep use steep terrain to avoid predators, but they are not so sure-footed as mountain goats and hence avoid sheer cliffs that a goat would not hesitate to use. In the winter months, sheep depend on areas of light snow cover where grasses are exposed for them to graze. This is one reason sheep are not found in the wet, heavy snow areas west of the Cascades. Other species also associated with— but not necessarily restricted to— the open, arid sage-covered eastern mountains, include mule deer, badger, coyote, golden eagle, ferruginous hawk, prairie falcon, red tail hawk, sage sparrow, canyon wren, black billed magpie, Belding's ground squirrel and sage thrasher.

Clockwise from top left:
Bighorn sheep ram. JAN WASSINK
Prairie falcons about to fledge.
GEORGE WUERTHNER
Young great horned owl. JAN WASSINK
Male sage grouse dance each spring on traditional strutting grounds called leks. JEFF FOOTT

33

Critters of the Forest Crown

In the forested areas of the state— the Cascades, Siskiyous, Coast Range and upper elevations of the Blue Mountain complex— we find an entirely different mix of wildlife. Some species like the coyote roam everywhere from grasslands to dense forests, but many others like the marten are much more closely associated with forested habitat. The marten is usually found in mature forests, and as this heavy tree cover has been logged, the marten has become increasingly rare in Oregon.

Marten are frequently trapped for their beautiful fur, which is a rich dark brown on top and often orange around the throat. The same animal in Europe is known as the sable. These animals are members of the weasel family, thus are long and slender with shining, beady eyes and like weasels, they tend to be curious. I have had a number of martens approach me in the forest darting from tree to stump and back to tree, all the while sizing me up from each vantage point. This inquisitiveness is perhaps one reason marten are easy to capture and very vulnerable to a skillful trapper.

Marten do most of their hunting at night, preying on pikas, voles, squirrels, rabbits and mountain beaver. They are quite at home in trees chasing squirrels, or wandering on the forest floor after voles and rabbits. I once watched a marten hunting in a rock slide for pikas, but the oddest place I ever met a marten was on a glacier. I have also found their scat loaded with wild strawberries and huckleberries during the summer.

Marten are shy and it is good fortune indeed to see this elusive creature, but almost anyone who spends time in the forests of the Coast Range or Cascades is bound to come upon the chickaree or Douglas squirrel. These active dark brown-gray animals inhabit Sitka spruce, Douglas fir and lodgepole pine forests and eat seeds from cones, pollen cones and mushrooms. Squirrels carrying mushrooms look particularly comical as they bounce along with a prize morsel almost as big their own bodies.

Conifer cones are industriously gathered in the autumn and stored in hollow logs or underground caches for winter use. The squirrel often hides many more cones than it will ever use and some of these cones will eject their seeds and subsequently sprout, generating a new forest to provide cones for future generations of squirrels. The chickaree often has a favorite log upon which it shreds cones to extract the seeds. These squirrel middens are recognizable by the piles of cone scales and descaled cores, which look something like miniature corn ears.

Top: Pine marten. TOM AND PAT LEESON
Above: Chickaree, or Douglas squirrel. GEORGE WUERTHNER
Right: Pikas cure hay for the winter. TOM AND PAT LEESON

Chickarees are particularly vocal. Their "burr" calls reverberate through the woods whenever these alert creatures spot anything amiss. Many a hunter has had his silent stalk ruined by the raucous warnings of these forest busybodies. Territorial disputes between squirrels usually amount to no more than a loud "shouting" match as each squirrel scolds the other, although at times one squirrel will almost blindly chase another from tree to tree. I was once sitting quietly in a forest, when one squirrel chasing another ran right over my legs without even noticing my presence until I jumped. The chase stopped and each squirrel scurried towards the nearest tree.

Chickarees are active in the day, but the flying squirrel, active at night, is rarely seen. The only flying squirrel I've ever observed poked its head out of a cavity in an old dead snag that I was drumming with a stick. The squirrel, perhaps awakened from its daytime slumber, looked out, jumped from its hole, and sailed safely to a nearby snag where it disappeared into another cavity. Flying squirrels don't really fly. Rather they glide, using as sails the loose skin attached to their legs, and may travel 150 feet at a rate of six feet per second.

In summer the flying squirrel's diet is 100 percent underground fungi. They help to disperse the spores of these valuable forest plants. This squirrel also has a fondness for meat and as a result winds up dead in traps meant to catch a marten or weasel. While out foraging for fungi on the forest floor, flying squirrels fall prey to the spotted owl.

Right: Black bears come in several color phases—including cinnamon, and brown as pictured here.
JAN WASSINK

Facing page: Roosevelt elk (seen here) are common in the dense coniferous forests west of the Cascades, while Rocky Mountain elk inhabit the east slope of the Cascades and the Blue Mountains.
TOM AND PAT LEESON

Large Mammals of the Forest Floor

Oregon once had two species of bears, the grizzly and black, but the last grizzly was seen in Wallowa County in 1931. Black bears, on the other hand, are very numerous, particularly in the Coast and Cascade Ranges, but are found in all major mountain areas of the state.

Black bears come in a variety of color phases. In Oregon these animals are sometimes brown, or reddish brown, giving rise to reports of grizzlies because many people assume all black bears are black and all grizzlies are brown. Although fur color is an unreliable identification characteristic for either bear, there are a few distinct differences between the two species. Black bears have short claws, usually less than an inch in length, while the grizzly has four-inch claws. Black bears also have narrow faces, longer snouts and lack the characteristic shoulder humps of grizzlies.

In Oregon, black bears eat just about anything they can find, from berries to picnic lunches: insects, carrion, and even spawned-out salmon are common foods. Some bears also strip the bark from trees to obtain the sugary cambium layer. This habit can kill the tree— and the bear— some timber companies have hired hunters to

Spotted Owl Primer

© GARY BRAASCH

Until the last decade, the northern spotted owl was a virtually unknown species. The first record of it in the Pacific Northwest did not occur until 1892, and the bird was considered rare throughout its range. It would still be an obscure species if it were not for its proclivity for old-growth forests. Studies conducted in the 1970s found that the owl was actually quite common throughout its range, but is declining at a rate of 1.1 percent a year as the last remaining old-growth forests are harvested. Current projections suggest that the northern spotted owl will be extinct over its entire range within 20 to 30 years.

An estimated 1,000 to 1,200 spotted owls live in Oregon today, but the species is already extinct in the northern coast range, where nearly all the old growth that survived early fires has been cut. Virtually no spotted owl habitat exists on private timberlands since private companies have completely cut the millions of acres they control. Thus the future of the spotted owl is tied to federal land management practices, principally those on U. S. Forest Service lands.

As of late 1986, the Forest Service had proposed protecting habitat for 550 pairs on all national forests within the northern spotted owl's range in Washington, Oregon

and northern California. Of the 550 sites proposed for protection, 392 are on lands unsuitable for timber harvest. According to the best estimates this will not halt the decline, but merely slow it, and the bird is likely to slide into extinction within the next century. The northern spotted owl seems to need a multilayered canopy, numerous dead and dying trees, and the abundance of snags and fallen logs of old-growth forests. Research in Oregon has shown that 98 percent of the locations for spotted owls over an 11-year period were in old-growth forests and that owls were 12 times more abundant in these habitats than in young second-growth forests.

The owl depends upon the old-growth forests in several ways. First, the dense canopy provides thermal regulation for the bird. In summer the shade keeps the animal cool and in winter the big old trees, with their large branches and sheltering boles, provide dry, warm roosting habitat necessary for survival in the cool, rainy winter. Perhaps for this reason spotted owls nest almost exclusively in large dead and dying trees. The most typical nest site is a cavity previously excavated by other old-growth-dependent species such as the pileated woodpecker. Lastly, the spotted owl's major prey species

destroy bark-stripping bears.

Black bears normally hibernate, even those living along the coast where temperatures are mild year-round. The hibernation is really just a deep sleep and bears can be aroused any time during their slumber. During the mid-winter sleep new cubs are born to pregnant females. The cubs are tiny, virtually hairless, and weigh less than a pound, but they grow rapidly and by the time they are a year old they may weigh 70 to 80 pounds. Cubs usually den with their mother the first winter, but are on their own after the second summer.

The elk is Oregon's largest land mammal. There are two sub-species: the Roosevelt and the Rocky Mountain elk. The Roosevelt elk has heavy, crowning antlers compared to the more spreading and less massive Rocky Mountain form, and tends to be slightly bigger in body and darker in color. The Roosevelt sub-species once roamed from Vancouver Island south into the coastal portions of northern California, while the Rocky Mountain elk was centered in Montana, Idaho, Wyoming and Colorado, and its natural range reached only into eastern Oregon. Due to transplants the Rocky Mountain form is now found on

are other denizens of these lush forests: the northern flying squirrel, red back vole and brushy tailed wood rat.

Part of the reason the spotted owl is so vulnerable to extinction is that its recruitment rate, or the rate at which breeding-age adults are added to the population, is relatively low. Owls don't reach sexual maturity until three years of age, and even then, if they do breed, an average of only two eggs is produced per pair. Not all of those hatched survive to fledge. Once on their own, the young owls have an extremely low survival rate. In one study, 31 recently fledged juveniles were radio-tagged and all were dead within two years! Thus, dispersal is a major problem for the species and as its habitat becomes more and more fragmented the death rate of dispersing owls can be expected to rise.

As habitat is separated into small fragmented "islands," extinction is much more likely. Small populations regularly die out due to chance catastrophic events and random fluctuations in numbers. In addition, if these islands are separated from other islands, recolonization of suitable, but vacant, habitat is unlikely. It is this fragmentation of old-growth habitat that will cause the owl's extinction long before all the old-growth forests disappear.

Top: Mule deer are common east of the Cascades. DAN DAVIDSON
Above: Blacktail deer fawn.
JAN WASSINK
Right: Blacktail deer nursing fawns.
TOM AND PET LEESON

the east side of the Cascades and the two sub-species readily interbreed as the differences between them are slight.

As a consequence of over-hunting, elk were dramatically reduced throughout Oregon by the turn of the century. In 1910 Forest Service officials reported elk as very scarce in the Siskiyou and Siuslaw national forests, and only 15 head were reported on the old Crater and Cascade national forests, which covered most of the Cascade Range. Protective measures helped begin a slow recovery, so that by 1926 there were 436 elk on all the national forests of western Oregon. Restrictive hunting seasons, transplants, and the creation of forest openings by logging and fires, further boosted elk numbers so that today, there are an estimated 53,000 elk in northeast Oregon alone! Nevertheless, increasingly easy access, made possible by a rapidly expanding logging-road system, means there are few large escape areas for these animals and hunting pressures are beginning to have significant impact upon the state's elk herds.

Where elk are abundant, deer numbers usually decline, although the two will often be found on the same ranges. While elk tend to be grazers, deer are almost always browsers, and except for eating succulent green grass in the spring, they subsist on shrubs. This preference for shrubs is one reason cattle grazing has actually increased deer herds in some places. Due to cattle's grazing pressure on grasses, shrubs gain a competitive advantage and eventually replace grasses in many areas—a boon for deer.

Deer live throughout Oregon, with both mule deer (blacktail) and the whitetail species represented. The diminutive blacktail deer lives along the fringes of the dense coniferous forests west of the Cascades, while the bulkier mule deer is widespread throughout the sage-covered rangelands and pine forests east of the Cascades. There are two sub-species of whitetail deer in Oregon, but they are relatively rare and confined to riparian zones along the lower Columbia and Snake rivers—seldom seen in the mountains.

Along the coast, deer remain in the same home range year-round. In the higher portions of the Cascades and the mountains of eastern Oregon, severe winter weather drives deer from lush, summer sub-alpine pastures to lowland winter ranges. The availability of winter range often sets the upper limits on deer population size.

Deer are by far the game animal most popular with Oregon hunters, and the annual hunting season is a

frenzied and cherished time for many people. Although many hunters believe predators kill a large number of deer each year, outside of the wilderness areas far more deer die on the roadsides than are killed by any other cause. In one study of 11,000 deer, more than 66.3 percent of the deaths, not counting legal hunting, were caused by collision with automobiles and trains.

Since wolves were eliminated from Oregon by early settlers and ranchers, the major predator on deer and elk is the mountain lion. Lions were killed for bounty from 1843 until 1961, when the bounty system was repealed by the state legislature. In 1967 the animal was listed as a game animal, thus subject to regulation by hunting seasons and bag limits. Mountain lions live throughout Oregon in every mountain range, and the areas with the largest deer herds usually have a correspondingly high lion population. Unlike the wolf, which hunts by running down its prey, the lion hunts by stealth and surprise, usually capturing prey after a short burst of speed.

Mountain lions stake out territories and the ranges of resident males do not overlap, although male territories will often overlap several female ranges. Young animals must wander until they find a vacant territory to occupy and it is often these young, inexperienced lions that create problems with livestock owners. For years, the mountain lion was listed as a predator and killed on sight, but studies suggest that it may be wiser to allow a

Left: Mountain lions prey primarily on deer—and an occasional porcupine. TOM AND PAT LEESON
Above: Great gray owls are relatively uncommon in Oregon, although they are found in the meadow and timber country southeast of the Cascades south of Bend and in the Blue Mountains. JEFF FOOTT

Above: Yellow-bellied marmots are common in the rock piles of many Oregon mountains. JAN WASSINK
Right top: Mountain goats are found only in the Wallowa Mountains, where they were introduced. JAN WASSINK

Right bottom: The desert-dwelling kit fox is found in southeast Oregon. GEORGE WUERTHNER

territory to be occupied by a non–livestock-eating lion than to kill indiscriminately and have the vacant territory occupied by a different lion, which may prefer lamb-chops and veal to venison.

Research by Maurice Hornocker in Idaho found that a mature lion will kill a deer every 10 to 14 days. After making a kill the mountain lion buries the uneaten portion and remains in the area until it is consumed. Like most predators, mountain lions are opportunistic and will kill any animal they can catch, but old and young prey are usually easier to capture. One study of mountain lions in northeast Oregon showed that mule deer was the major prey species, although a few elk also were taken. Ten percent of the lions in this particular study had also eaten porcupines, without apparent ill effect.

Insects: Vital Link Between Plant and Animal Worlds

When most people think of forest animals, they conjure up images of squirrels, deer and bear. Virtually unseen and unnoticed are perhaps the most important forest animals, the thousands of invertebrate species like beetles, ants and spiders that help to bridge the gap between the plant and animal worlds. Without these critters to break down woody material, recycle nutrients, and provide food for many small rodents and birds, many higher organisms such as bears and deer might not exist.

One resident of the rotten logs on the forest floor is the carpenter ant. Both sexes of young adult ants are winged and leave the nest in spring to mate. The male dies after mating but the female may try to establish a new colony. She finds a cavity in a fallen tree and builds a brood cell, which is completely sealed and in which a number of eggs are laid. The eggs hatch in about 10 days and the new young feed on a special secretion exuded from the female's salivary glands. Each larva then spins a cocoon, pupates and changes into an adult within about 30 days, becoming the workers for the new ant colony.

Worker ants cut galleries through soft rotten wood, and the sawdust piles up outside the log. Indeed, these tiny windrows of wood fiber are one of the easiest ways to identify the location of an ant colony. The ants do not eat the wood, but instead capture caterpillars and other small insects, which are carried back to the colony.

Aphids are tiny insects that feed on plant leaves and produce a sweet secretion called honeydew, relished by the ants. To ensure a bountiful supply of honeydew the carpenter ants "ranch" aphids by sheltering aphid eggs

in their nests during the winter, and carrying in the proper plant leaves in the spring.

Ants provide several services useful to the forest. Their tunnels open the rotting log to penetration by other wood decomposers, such as fungi and bacteria. And they are food for many forest dwellers from the flicker to the black bear.

Fisheries Confront Progress

Besides providing room and board to a wide variety of terrestrial species, Oregon's mountains offer an abundance of habitat for the state's renowned fisheries. Native game fish include cutthroat, rainbow, and Dolly Varden trout. Introduced species include brook trout and brown trout. In addition to these year-round residents, a number of fish species are born in mountain waters, and migrate to the sea to grow to adulthood. They return to their natal streams to spawn. Oregon is home to steelhead (a sea-run rainbow trout), sea-run cutthroat trout, pink, chinook, coho, chum and sockeye salmon. Unfortunately for migratory species, dams have presented almost insurmountable obstacles. Most people believe that dams blocking upstream migration present the greatest barrier to salmon and steelhead, but it is actually the seaward journey of juvenile fish that causes the highest mortality when fish must pass through the slicing blades of turbines.

Due to the problems posed by dams, as well as continued degradation of waterways by grazing, logging, and agricultural uses such as irrigation, Oregon has turned increasingly to hatcheries to supplement or even replace wild, natural runs of fish. Beyond the operational costs

there are other drawbacks to this reliance on stocked fish. Wild fish are genetically adapted to the specific environmental conditions of their home streams and as a result often have much higher survival rates than hatchery fish. In addition, disease spreads easily under crowded hatchery conditions, posing the constant threat of major die-offs because of infection.

Research in Montana found that stocking hatchery fish into waters with wild populations actually resulted in dramatic declines in fish numbers. Hatchery fish compete with wild populations for existing habitat and food and since both of these are finite resources, the end result is that many trout starve or are so weakened that they succumb to other stresses. Because of this study, Oregon is beginning to question its reliance upon hatcheries and has designated some streams as wild fisheries.

As people have settled the lowlands and valleys, changing woodlands into subdivisions and grasslands into croplands, the mountains have remained the primary home and refuge for many wildlife species. Now, as more roads and developments advance into these last sanctuaries, many species are pushed into increasingly smaller and smaller patches of habitat. This fragmentation seriously jeopardizes their future. No one can say whether the spotted owl will be missed, any more than it appears that sharp tailed grouse, wolves or grizzlies— animals already extinct in Oregon— are missed. Nevertheless, with each extinction a bit of the magic and enchantment of the mountains will disappear and along with it, a part of Oregon's soul will be lost.

Left to right:
Steller's jay.
Mountain bluebird.
Western tanager.
JAN WASSINK PHOTOS

41

CHAPTER 6

The Cascades

Above: Broken Top Mountain and Sparks Lake near Bend. STEVE TERRILL

Right: Mt. Hood, Oregon's best-known mountain and highest peak, reflected in Lost Lake. PAT O'HARA

The name Cascades seems like an appropriate label for the high, snow-capped range that runs north-south across the entire state of Oregon. Tumbling off the steep western slopes of these mountains are hundreds of waterfalls and cataracts fed by the heavy winter rain and snowfall. It seems that there are few valleys where the sound, if not the sight, of rushing water is absent.

The Cascades were first mentioned by Captain Vancouver during his exploration of the Pacific Northwest coast in 1792, and several peaks— including Mt. Hood— were named by Vancouver or members of his expedition. But it appears that David Douglas, the botanist for whom the Douglas fir is named, was the first to use the name "Cascade" in reference to these snowy peaks. Other names for these high peaks followed, including Presidents Range (Mt. Jefferson named by Lewis and Clark still commemorates Thomas Jefferson), but the Cascades eventually became the accepted name.

The Cascades contain all of Oregon's mountains that rise above 10,000': Mt. Hood (11,245'), Mt. Jefferson (10,479'), South Sister (10,358'), North Sister (10,085'), and Middle Sister (10,047'). Four other peaks within the range exceed 9,000' and at least seven reach 8,000'. Except for the Columbia Gorge, no low passes exist in the entire Oregon portion of the range. Barlow at 4,155' and Wapinitia at 3,949' are the lowest passes, while the average height of the main crest is about 5,000'.

More than any other mountain range, the Cascades define what Oregon is today. The range stretches beyond the state's borders in an unbroken chain parallel to the Pacific Ocean from Lassen Peak in California north to Mt. Garibaldi in British Columbia. In Oregon, these mountains present a barrier that divides Oregon into two regions. To the west the climate is mild and wet, while beyond the range to the east are the arid, sunny, open spaces of eastern Oregon. Because of these climatic differences, the vegetation, fauna, and even human economic and settlement patterns differ.

Oregon's Cascades can be divided into two separate mountain ranges: the older Western Cascades and the New or High Cascades, both volcanic. Except for the occasional high peak that punctuates the High Cascades, these newer mountains are gentler than the older, heavily eroded Western Cascades. The Cascades began as a series of volcanoes some 50 million years ago, and volcanism is still shaping the range, as the eruption of Mt. St. Helens in Washington attests. No geologist would be surprised by new eruptions in the McKenzie and Santiam Pass areas or at Mt. McLoughlin to the south.

Born in Fire

The Western Cascades consist mostly of lava flows, volcanic mudflow deposits and layers of volcanic ash. The oldest rocks erupted about 50 million years ago from a chain of volcanoes that trended northeastward from the area southwest of Eugene to somewhere near Pendleton. The Ochoco Mountains are the eroded remains of some of those volcanoes. Such volcanic chains normally trend parallel to the coast, so it seems likely that the continental margin of 50 million years ago angled northeast through what is now western and central Oregon.

Mt. Jefferson in the Mt. Jefferson Wilderness has the conical shape of a stratovolcano. PAT O'HARA

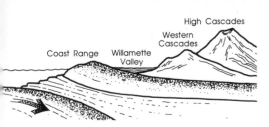

andesite lavas that built the conical stratovolcanoes that preside over the modern landscape of the Cascades.

When Mt. Mazama blew up to create Crater Lake, glowing pumice fragments poured out to the east and north for more than 20 miles and ash scattered over much of central Oregon—in places to a depth of 100'. Eruptions at Newberry Crater also added ash. The soils derived from these ash and pumice deposits have unique properties including limited ability to store heat, lack of heat radiation at night and slow heat transfer within the soil—all properties of good insulators, like the styrofoam used to make picnic coolers. As a result these soils are very cold and basins within the region become frost traps. Any opening, such as a meadow or clearcut, acts as a sink, collecting cold air from the surrounding uplands.

Young trees susceptible to frost cannot survive in these areas and regeneration is difficult, even for trees planted in reforestation projects. In addition, since heat transfer is slow, the soil surface heats to temperatures lethal to young seedlings on hot summer days. One of the few tree species able to tolerate these extremes is lodgepole pine. It is widespread throughout the region, especially in basins or pockets where cold air collects.

Some of the most recent eruptions and lava flows, estimated to be between 1,600 and 400 years old, are visible along Highway 242 at McKenzie Pass, just north of the Three Sisters. The Belknap volcano, a shield volcano, along with South Belknap and Little Belknap, erupted very fluid flows of basalt. These spread over the landscape in thin layers developing the low, uninspiring profiles typical of shield volcanoes. The Forest Service's Dee Wright Observatory sits on another younger lava flow erupted from the Yapoah Cone, three miles southeast of the highway. Scattered about the lava flows are stunted and scraggly-looking whitebark pine, mountain hemlock, lodgepole pine and Engelmann spruce all struggling to survive on the barren, hot moonscape surface.

Another area of recent volcanic activity is Lava Butte adjacent to Highway 97, 10 miles south of Bend. This cinder cone is part of a series of cones marking a 20-mile-long fissure that extends from the Newberry Crater. Once a cinder cone erupts, it is dead, so one is safe taking the paved road to the top of Lava Butte. Ponderosa pines cover its flanks, but a recent treeless, blocky, broken flow of basalt runs west toward the Deschutes River. There it has created Benham, Dillon and Lava Island falls.

Nearby are a number of other geologic attractions including the Lava River Cave, formed when a molten river

Later volcanic eruptions that continued until about 20 million years ago built the main mass of the Western Cascades, which parallels the present coastline through Oregon and Washington. Some of the old Western Cascade volcanic vents now contain granite intrusions, some of which mineralized their enclosing rock to emplace ore bodies such as the one that supported the Bohemia gold mining district.

Volcanic activity in the Cascades ceased sometime around 20 million years ago, about the time the eruptions that built the Columbia Plateau began. Then, as the Columbia Plateau volcanoes became extinct about 10 million years ago, a new chain of vents began building the modern High Cascades. In most areas, those eruptions began with a long series of basalt lava flows that filled the stream valleys, then built broad shield volcanoes. Then, the volcanoes began to erupt more viscous

of lava from Newberry Crater cooled on its outer surface while the warmer, still-liquid rock on the inside drained away, leaving a tube. The inside of the cave maintains an ambient temperature of 40 degrees year-round and ice persists even through the hot summer days. In the same vicinity is the Lava Cast Forest, where lava flows spilled into an existing forest and cooled around the bases of live trees forming exact impressions of them.

New magma is not far beneath the surface in many places, as numerous hot springs throughout the Cascades indicate. The city of Klamath Falls sits on top of one of these hot spots; heated springs once flowed in town. Many of the public buildings and a few homes are heated by natural steam and hot water obtained by drilling very shallow wells. Newberry Crater is one of the hottest spots in the Cascades. A 3,000' test well drilled by the U.S. Geological Survey found water heated to 550 degrees. In anticipation of geothermal development,

more than 250,000 acres of Forest Service lands outside of the caldera have been leased to speculators who hope to cash in on any activity.

Glacial Scars

Although fire may have created the Cascades, ice gave many of the higher peaks their present features. The Ice Ages came and went again and again. At the height of the glacial advance, nearly all areas above 5,000' on the Cascade crest were covered with glacial ice. Valley glaciers streamed down the mountain canyons to elevations as low as 3,500'. After the mantling sheet of ice melted, smaller glaciers continued to rework the higher summits. A glacier occupied a cirque on the northeast flank of McLoughlin less than a century ago.

As a result of glacial sculpting many of the higher reaches of the range have deeply gouged valleys, cirque

Left: Mt. Thielsen's pointed profile is a clue to its age. Severe glacial erosion for millions of years has reduced this volcano from the typically conical shape of young volcanoes into this finger-like feature. JEFF GNASS
Above: Lava flows at McKenzie Pass are younger than 2,000 years old and the slow process of soil formation inhibits colonization by plants such as this manzanita.
GEORGE WUERTHNER

45

Crater Lake National Park

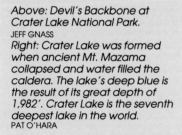

Above: Devil's Backbone at Crater Lake National Park.
JEFF GNASS
Right: Crater Lake was formed when ancient Mt. Mazama collapsed and water filled the caldera. The lake's deep blue is the result of its great depth of 1,982'. Crater Lake is the seventh deepest lake in the world.
PAT O'HARA

Crater Lake is Oregon's only national park, and vividly displays evidence of the cataclysmic events that created it. About 6,600 years ago Mount Mazama, a high Cascade peak, erupted as it had many times before, but this time the release of magma was so great the mountain collapsed on itself and left behind a six-mile-wide caldera that eventually filled with water to form Crater Lake. Mount Mazama was a strato-volcano similar to other high Cascade mountains like Mount Hood and Mount Rainier. Geologists estimate that it may have been more than 12,000' in elevation, which would have made it the highest peak in Oregon, although by the time of the final explosion its height may have been substantially reduced by previous eruptions.

Before this last major eruption, the mountain had built up a gently sloping cone and had even buried one other older volcano in the process. This remnant is now exposed in the caldera and called the Phantom Cone. Phantom Ship, visible as a tiny island in the lake, was probably a lava dike intruded into this cone. As the mountain grew, other smaller cones built up on its flanks, and Mount Scott, which now rises 8,926' above the eastern shore of the lake, was one of these parasitic cones.

Glaciers covered the mountain's flanks, as they now cover other Cascade peaks. A number of valleys, such as Munson Valley and Kerr Notch, as well as the western face of Mount Scott, bear unmistakable evidence of past glaciation including cirques and U-shaped valleys. Most of these glaciers, however, had retreated and melted away several thousand years prior to the last explosion.

At the time of the eruption, rhyolite magma, high in silica and thus very viscous, plugged the volcano. Steam trapped in the rock caused this molten rock to boil over

and flow down the flanks of the mountain like glowing avalanches, some of which crept down existing valleys for miles. One traveled 40 miles along the Rogue River valley, burning everything in its path. This mixture of pumice, ash and steam was so hot, it welded together rock fragments to produce the welded ash flows we see today along the sides of the caldera.

In addition to these fiery rock rivers, the mountain blew tons of ash and pumice so high into the sky that it settled over what are today eight western states, and Canadian provinces as far away as Saskatchewan. Because the predominent wind was from the west, most of this tremendous outpouring of ash settled to the east and north. This ash explosion created the pumice soils that now blanket the slopes east of the Cascades, making for special micro-climate conditions in which it is difficult for many plants to colonize and survive.

After emptying its magma chambers, the mountain collapsed, rather than blowing away its entire summit as many people used to think. Even after this collapse, new cones grew up from the floor of the crater, one of which we see today as Wizard Island.

The empty caldera eventually filled with rain water and snowmelt to a depth of 1,932', making it the deepest lake in the United States and the seventh deepest in the world. Even in the winter, the lake seldom freezes because of its great depth. Water below 328' remains a constant 38 degrees year-round. Heat given off by this relatively "warm" water rises to the surface and prevents the formation of ice except under unusual conditions, so that, even in winter, a deep-blue lake surrounded by snow-covered slopes greets the visitor.

Left: Wind-sheared pine on Mt. Scott, the highest peak in Crater Lake National Park.
GEORGE WUERTHNER
Above: Pinnacles at Crater Lake National Park result from the differential erosion of volcanic ash.
PAT O'HARA

amphitheaters, and moraine-dammed lakes— all features characteristic of glacial activity. Many of the higher peaks, such as Mt. Hood, North, Middle and South Sister and Mt. Jefferson, still bear active glaciers on their flanks, and other peaks like Mt. Scott, Mt. Washington, Three Finger Jack and Diamond Peak still bear the scars of past glaciation, including cirques and moraines. The largest glacier in Oregon, the Collier, lies on the north flank of Middle Sister.

The amount of glacial erosion provides a clue to the age of major Cascade mountains. For example, Mt. Thielsen, Mt. Washington, Union Peak, and Three Finger Jack were eroded severely by glaciers into pyramid-shaped peaks known as horns, after Switzerland's famous Matterhorn. Horn peaks are created when three or four glaciers on opposing sides of a mountain carve cirques and leave between them a steep angular pinnacle. All these volcanoes were extinct by the beginning of the last major glaciation, and thus retain their extensively eroded appearance. Mountains that erupted more recently, such as South Sister, retain their typical volcanic cone shape.

These high peaks sharply divide climatic conditions on either side of the range. Salem, west of the mountains, receives 40" of annual precipitation, while higher on the western slopes, 100" or more fall, mostly as snow. Madras, east of the mountains, receives only 9.6" of

Far left: The view north from the top of South Sister to Middle and North Sisters, Three Sisters Wilderness, near Bend. GEORGE WUERTHNER
Left: Heavy snowfall is characteristic of the Cascades; snowmelt throughout the summer provides a steady supply of water for industry, agriculture, domestic uses and recreation. LARRY ULRICH
Below: Mt. Washington reflected in Big Lake. STEVE TERRILL
Right: Three Finger Jack at sunrise in Mt. Jefferson Wilderness. JEFF GNASS

precipitation in an average year. Even the snow east of the crest is drier, as skiers at Bachelor Butte by Bend constantly remind their west-slope counterparts.

Reflecting the climatic conditions, major tree species and their associations differ on opposite sides of this range. There are few places in the United States where the contrasts are so apparent in such a short distance. These Cascade coniferous forests are among the most magnificent in the world in terms of size, extent and diversity of species. Many of the low-elevation forests are privately owned by the large timber companies, while most of the mid to high-elevation forests are national forests.

Above: Ponderosa pine often forms extensive pure stands along the east slope of the Cascades, as seen here on the Winema National Forest.
LARRY ULRICH
Right: Logging in the Cascades. "Tree wars" have developed over logging of old-growth timber stands—pitting those bent on saving the old trees for aesthetic and ecological value against those who see the immediate employment opportunities of timber harvest.
GEORGE WUERTHNER

Extensive areas of the eastern slopes are covered by vast stands of some of the most exquisite old-growth ponderosa pine forests in the West that support mills in Bend, Redmond and other towns along the eastern fringe of the mountains. Until recently, wildfires regularly burned through these forests at five- to 20-year intervals, keeping them open with few understory shrubs. Today, as a result of fire suppression, the forests are overstocked and unhealthy, smothered in their own growth.

Lodgepole pine is common on the pumice soils east of the Cascades and in the Paulina Mountains. It dominates the basins where cold air collects. Lodgepole, like ponderosa pine, evolved with wildfire and pine beetles and actually depends upon these natural thinning agents to ensure its continued survival on a given site. Beetle infestations occur where trees are not regularly thinned by fire or natural mortality, but once the stand is opened by the death of less vigorous trees, the remaining trees are able to resist beetle infections and the epidemic subsides.

The Deschutes National Forest surrounding Bend is currently in the midst of a beetle epidemic. Forest managers propose massive roading and logging of beetle infested stands over the next 15 years. Unfortunately, lodgepole pine has limited market value, so to cover the road-building, administration and other costs, many of these sales will be subsidized by taxpayers' money. It may be far cheaper to allow the beetle epidemic to run its course, than to spend money attempting to do what the beetle will do anyway.

West of the Cascades is the domain of the giant old-growth Douglas fir, western hemlock and western red cedar forests. Interspersed along riparian zones and in the forest understory are vine and bigleaf maple, both of which add fall color to these west-slope timber stands. Some of the oldest Douglas firs reach ages of nearly a thousand years and are considered valuable not only for their part in long-term nutrient cycling, stream-bank stability, wildlife habitat (more than 200 species of wildlife rely on old growth for their home and food), but also for their majestic beauty in these mossy, cathedral-like groves.

Diverse Forests

"Tree wars" have developed in Oregon, as those bent on logging the old growth battle those set on preservation. Tactics used by both sides include the standard legal methods as well as more direct action such as blockading roads and holding demonstrations. In some cases, people have stood in front of bulldozers or chained themselves to trees to discourage loggers.

In moister, low-elevation sites, one finds the grand fir, often growing with western hemlock and Douglas fir and at times ponderosa pine. In mid-elevation forests of the southern Cascades above 4,000' are regal stands of Shasta red fir, a beautiful tree with a rich cinnamon bark and tall straight boles. North of Crater Lake this fir is replaced by noble fir, and the two are so similar that many foresters consider them the same species. At the higher elevation subalpine regions, one may encounter several other firs, including silver fir and subalpine fir.

Members of the fir genus, *Abies*, can be identified by their habit of holding cones upright on the branch, instead of downward as do most other conifers. Fir cones usually disintegrate on the trees, so unless you are lucky enough to find a cone dropped by a squirrel or broken off in a windstorm, you rarely find whole fir cones on the ground.

Other mid-elevation forests include scattered occurrences of western white pine, incense cedar, Engelmann spruce, and in the southern Cascades, knobcone and sugar pine. These species are seldom found in pure stands, but occur intermixed with other trees. On the east slope, especially north of McKenzie Pass, are scattered stands of western larch, a species quite common in the Blue and Wallowa mountains that reaches its western limits here along the east slope of the Cascades.

At the highest elevations of the Cascades one may encounter the Alaska yellow cedar, as well as mountain hemlock and whitebark pine. The pine tends to be limited to drier sites, while the hemlock and cedar are more common in wetter locations.

Mountains Put to Use

Logging is one of the major economic activities on both sides of the Cascades. Nearly all tree species can be used for the wood products industry, but the most important trees are ponderosa pine east of the Cascades, and Douglas fir west of the crest. Nearly every small town has a mill and on weekdays the sound of logging trucks on mountain highways is a nearly continuous roar.

So diverse are the Cascades habitats that these mountains are home to nearly every wildlife species found in Oregon, with the exception of ocean-dependent animals. Antelope, for instance, occasionally roam from their wintering grounds by Fort Rock and pass through dense forests to summer by Klamath Marsh, or even on the eastern slopes by Crater Lake National Park.

Along the crest of the Cascades blacktail deer from the west slope mix and sometimes hybridize with mule deer common to the east. The same mixing of sub-species occurs with Roosevelt elk of the dense west-slope forests and Rocky Mountain elk of the range's eastern flanks. Many of the elk that one sees on the east side of the Cascades in summer migrate through 10' of snow in early spring from their winter range on the west slope. A few elk herds also winter on the High Desert in the Fort Rock Valley. The Cascades are not great elk country, lacking meadows in their generally dry, shrub-free forests, which provide little food. According to Oregon Fish and Game biologists, the very high national forest road densities— as much as 11 miles of logging road per square mile— eliminate elk security cover, and the animals are harassed by too many hunters as a result of the easy access.

The rugged features of Mt. Jefferson or the Three Sisters seem like ideal habitat for climbing animals like mountain goats and bighorn sheep, but both are absent. The Cascades are probably too wet for bighorns, which prefer drier, open country. But there seems to be sufficient goat habitat, so why aren't they here? The best answer is that goats are not great swimmers and the closest mountain goat populations occur north of the Columbia River in Washington. Presumably the river has prevented them from colonizing the Oregon Cascades.

Predators of deer and elk once included wolves, grizzly bears, mountain lions and black bears. Wolves and grizzlies were exterminated decades ago, but the black bear and mountain lion still abound. Another wide–ranging Cascade predator is the wolverine. No accurate population estimates are available for these elusive animals, who are known to travel a hundred miles in a week.

Not all species suffer from human rearrangement of the environment. Crane Prairie Reservoir near Bend has one of the highest osprey nesting densities found in North America. The population peaked about 10 years ago when some 150 to 175 pairs nested on the lake, but since that time, the number has dropped to 35 to 50 pairs as a result of losses in old nest snags, also perhaps because of pesticide poisoning in Mexico and South America, where these birds winter.

Of the Cascade peaks, Mt. Hood is undoubtedly the best known. The elegant pyramid-shaped mountain just south of the Columbia gorge is the highest peak in Oregon, rising to a height of 11,245' and made even more impressive by the lack of competing high peaks nearby. For many travelers of the dust-covered Oregon Trail, the sight of the snow-clad volcanic peak signaled the end of

A hiker is dwarfed by an old-growth Douglas fir stand along the Salmon River on the Mt. Hood National Forest. The abundance of fallen logs is one important feature of old-growth forests. The logs provide structural and nutritional stability.
GEORGE WUERTHNER

51

Top: Timberline Lodge on Mt. Hood, a national historic site built during the 1930s as a public works project, is now a ski lodge. CRAIG TUTTLE
Above: Indian paintbrush and penstemon on Mt. Hood. STEVE TERRILL

a long journey and a promise of green meadows and forested slopes beyond. The first attempt at climbing its glacier-mantled summit was made in 1845. Thousands now climb it each year, making it the world's second most-climbed snow peak behind Japan's Mt. Fuji.

On the southeast slope of the mountain is the famous Timberline Lodge and ski area. Timberline Lodge, now a national historic site, was built by the Civilian Conservation Corps during the 1930s. More than 500 craftsmen and artists labored on the project, completed in 1937.

Encircling the mountain is the 36-mile-long Timberline trail, part of which passes through the 15-by-six-mile Mt. Hood Wilderness. Traversing the wilderness is the Pacific Crest Trail, which follows the spine of mountains from the Canadian to Mexican border. More than 400 miles of its length lies in Oregon.

The Cascades contain 17 designated wilderness areas, including the Three Sisters Wilderness— at 285,202 acres, the second largest in Oregon. But most are much smaller, like the 7,500-acre Middle Santiam, which is less than five miles long and two miles wide. Nearly every major volcanic peak is surrounded by a wilderness area, including Mt. Hood, Mt. Jefferson, Mt. Washington, the Three Sisters, Diamond Peak, Mt. Thielsen and Mt. McLoughlin. These areas, as well as hundreds of hiking trails, campgrounds, numerous lakes, and rivers, and ski areas, make this region one of the most popular tourist and recreation areas in the state. Tourism and the recreation industry in the Cascades-Portland area generated more than a billion dollars in 1985.

In 1986 the Columbia Gorge was designated a National Scenic Area to be administered by the Forest Service. Created by the downcutting of the Columbia River, which existed before the Cascades, the gorge is 85 miles in length. Waterfalls like Multnomah, fourth highest in the country, drape the walls of side canyons. Bonneville Dam, one of several major dams on the Columbia, is at the upper end of the canyon.

At present only one national park, Crater Lake, graces the Oregon Cascades. Many feel the range's beauty, recreational opportunities, and extensive geological and biological wonders like the old-growth Douglas fir groves, merit national protection. There has been some discussion of a Cascades Volcano National Park to encompass the entire crest of the range from Mt. Hood south to Mt. McLoughlin. The park would include a good proportion of the Pacific Crest Trail and many existing wilderness areas, all the remaining roadless areas on either side of the range, and developed recreation sites.

Southeast of Bend is a group of volcanic cones and peaks known as the Paulina Mountains, with Newberry Crater at its center. Paulina Peak, the highest point in this volcanic complex at 7,984', has a road to its top. On a clear day one can see nearly all the high peaks of the Oregon Cascades.

The Paulinas are related in age and structure to the High Cascades and, as in the High Cascades, volcanic eruptions have occurred here within the last 2,000 years. The Newberry volcano is the largest shield volcano in Oregon — nearly 25 miles across. Like Crater Lake, the five-mile-wide crater collapsed after the volcano erupted an enormous volume of ash and pumice. The crater contains two lakes: Paulina and East Lake. Approximately 1,300 years ago a mass of rhyolite magma flowed down the inside wall of the caldera to form a frozen river of obsidian, or volcanic glass. The Obsidian Flow is seen from the summit of Paulina Peak. From this perspective, the mass of obsidian looks like a black glacier, complete with crevasses.

The Paulinas were named for Chief Paulina, who terrorized settlers, trappers, and others daring to enter central and eastern Oregon in the 1860s. Although the Army pursued him he always managed to avoid capture, and died rather ignobly in 1867 when a rancher shot him while he was stealing cattle. Yet, despite his reputation as a renegade, it seems more landmarks in Oregon are named for him than for anyone else. There are Paulina Peak, the Paulina Mountains, Paulina Lake, Paulina Creek, Paulina Prairie, and a community named Paulina.

Far left: Waterfalls are abundant within the Cascades. Multnomah Falls, second highest in the U.S., cascades down cliffs along the Columbia Gorge National Scenic Area.
Above: Upper Proxy Falls in Oregon's Three Sisters Wilderness.
Left: Horsetail Falls in Columbia Gorge National Scenic Area.
GEORGE WUERTHNER PHOTOS

Sunrise from Paulina Peak looking over Newberry Crater toward the distant snow-covered high peaks of the Cascades. GEORGE WUERTHNER

A Harvest, Not a Home

Few Indians lived in the Paulina Mountains or in any of Oregon's mountains year-round. Most lived where most of the area's residents live today— in the lowlands on either side of the range. The Indians only occasionally crossed the mountains for trade.

Europeans who first ventured into Oregon were in the fur trade and their travel centered on the natural corridor afforded by the Columbia River. The British scouted the Pacific Northwest coast early on, but the American expedition of Lewis and Clark in 1804-1806 was the first white party to actually cross the Cascades via the Columbia Gorge, into what would later be Oregon.

On the heels of Lewis and Clark were a number of other explorers and fur traders vying for control of the strategic Columbia. British fur trader David Thompson canoed the entire length of the Columbia in 1811, only to find that the American Pacific Fur Company, founded by John Jacob Astor, had already built a fort at Astoria. Un-

fortunately for Astor, the venture never panned out and the fort was sold to the British Northwest Fur Company in 1813. However, Astor's men did contribute significantly to the later settlement of the west by pioneering the South Pass route over the Rockies that became the Oregon Trail.

The Northwest Fur Company eventually merged with its chief rival, the Hudson's Bay Company, and many Northwesters joined the ranks of their former business competitors. The Company, as it was known, established its headquarters at Fort Vancouver on the north bank of the Columbia, upstream from the mouth of the Willamette River.

The high Cascade peaks formed an almost impassable barrier for both the Indians and the early white settlers. People traveling through Oregon went north and south following the main valleys like the Willamette, but few attempted crossing the high, densely forested range. One of the first whites to cross the Cascades was Finan McDonald, a brigade leader with the Hudson's Bay Company. After crossing the range in December of 1825, McDonald rendezvoused with another Hudson's Bay employee, Peter Skene Ogden (for whom Ogden, Utah is named) on the Deschutes River, which the fur trapping French Canadians named "Riviere des Chutes" for its many falls and rapids. The names of other mountain men and fur traders now grace Cascade features, including McKenzie Pass and the McKenzie River, named for 300-pound Donald McKenzie, a fur brigade leader who first explored the Willamette Valley in 1812 while in the employ of the Astoria party. Another large man, Dr. John McLoughlin, chief factor of the Hudson's Bay Company at Fort Vancouver between 1824 and 1846, is commemorated by Mt. McLoughlin in the southern Cascades. McLoughlin is often considered the father of Oregon for his generosity and kindness to early travelers, even competing fur company employees. He demonstrated the farming and lumbering possibilities of the region by building the first sawmill and flourmill, and developed the earliest agricultural enterprises in the Pacific Northwest. He left the fur trade in 1846 and settled in Oregon City, where he died in 1857.

Many of the earliest settlers of the Willamette Valley were former Hudson's Bay Company employees. French Prairie, north of present-day Salem, was named for the French-Canadians who farmed the area after leaving the service of the company. In the 1830s, several missionary groups found the region ideal for farming and began to promote the Willamette region for American settlement.

In 1843, the first large contingent of Americans, more than 900, arrived on the Oregon Trail.

Subdued by Trails and Roads

In an era of modern highways and air transportation, it is difficult to imagine the almost insurmountable obstacle the Cascades presented to early travelers. The only low-elevation passage in the entire range is the Columbia Gorge, where travel by boat was treacherous at best. The first immigrants built rafts at The Dalles and then floated down the river to Fort Vancouver. For many it was the most perilous part of the entire 2,000-mile journey. More than a handful of people lost their possessions or their lives in the swirling currents.

To avoid this water route, an 1844 group of Oregon Trail immigrants attempted to cross the Cascades south of Mt. Hood. They wound up abandoning their wagons and rode their exhausted livestock out of the mountains. One member of this party, Samuel Barlow, proposed to the newly formed Oregon provisional legislature that a road be built across the mountains. Barlow declared: "God never made a mountain that he had not made a place for some man to go over it or under it. I am going to hunt for that place..."

The first wagon trail across the Cascades, constructed by Barlow in 1845 and known as the Barlow Road, avoided the gorge by climbing around the southern flank of Mt. Hood. The road was hacked from the dense evergreen forests, from Gate Creek near Tygh Valley, to Government Camp, thence along the Zig Zag River to Sandy and Portland. In its first year of operation more than 145 wagons, 1,559 horses, mules and cattle passed over the road.

Other trails and roads over the Cascades followed, such as the Scott Trial, which passes over today's McKenzie Pass. So steep were certain parts of the trail that teams of 26 oxen were required to pull a single wagon. Hogg Pass, now called Santiam, was discovered in 1859 by a hunter, Andrew Wiley, who located a road through the area in the 1860s. The Linn County Company, a private enterprise, completed improvement on what was known as the Wiley Pass Road in 1865 and 1866. For its work, the company received alternate sections of land, as the railroads later would. Many of today's highways follow the routes these early road builders pioneered across the mountains.

Gold was discovered in Oregon in 1851, but the volcanic rocks of the Cascades were poor prospects. A few small discoveries were made in the Western Cascades at Blue

River, Bohemia and other locations where small pockets of mineralized rock were close to the surface. Without the impetus of mining, however, the Cascades remained unexplored and unsettled.

In the 1860s and 1870s stockmen drove sheep and cattle to the high country for grazing, but as the extent of these mountain meadows was limited, even this activity did not lead to significant development. Many ranches were established in the grass-pine zone along the eastern fringe of the mountains and in the open prairies of the Willamette Valley, but the mountains proper remained little visited. When tourists finally reached the Cascades, new resorts and developments began popping up at scenic areas, particularly at Mt. Hood and Crater Lake.

The Cascades are Oregon's best known, and in many people's minds, its most beautiful mountain range. If current efforts to preserve most of the range as a national park are successful, these mountains may continue to be both beautiful and appreciated.

The depressions cut into the slopes of Broken Top Mountain in the Cascades are examples of glacial cirques. GEORGE WUERTHNER

55

CHAPTER 7

The Blue Mountains

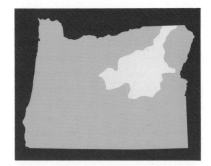

Frosted rabbitbrush along the John Day River. GEORGE WUERTHNER

Strawberry Mountain from John Day River Valley near Prairie City.
LARRY ULRICH

Oregon's Rockies

Upon my first rambles in the Eagle Cap Wilderness of northeast Oregon's Wallowa Mountains, I was impressed with their resemblance to the northern Rockies, with steep glaciated valleys and cirque-filled peaks. The Wallowas are high enough to break above timber-line, but just barely, and the forest itself is unlike those found in western Oregon. The trees were smaller, although large by Rocky Mountain standards, and the mix of western larch, Douglas fir, ponderosa pine, sub-alpine fir and lodgepole could be found in Northern Rockies canyons. If boundaries were not based solely on political happenstance, the Wallowa Mountains and most of Northeast Oregon would be considered part of the Rocky Mountains, and indeed many geographers consider this region to be the western extension of the northern Rockies.

In many ways the early human history reflects this connection to the Rockies. Tribes like the Nez Perce and Cayuse who lived in this region began to make annual hunts for bison on the Montana plains after they acquired the horse in the early 1700s. Their dress and many religious beliefs were similar to those of the plains tribes they encountered in the Rockies.

Over trails created by the seasonal movement of the aboriginal inhabitants, the first white trappers, particularly those working for the Hudson's Bay Company, entered the Blue Mountains region looking for furs. Peter Skene Ogden was one of these brigade leaders and his party trapped the Crooked, Powder, John Day and other river basins beginning in 1824. Later, these travel routes became the trails that brought settlers into Oregon. Today Interstate 84 passes through the Blue Mountains from La Grande to Pendleton following the Oregon Trail Route; Emigrant Hill above Pendleton was named in honor of the pioneers who passed this way. Although most Oregon Trail travelers continued on to the Willamette Valley, a few settled in this region, ranching the grasslands that fringed the Ochocos, Blues, and other mountains. But as in the Rockies, it was gold that provided the real impetus for settlement beginning in 1861.

Towns like Baker and John Day got their starts during the early heyday of mining, and the feeling of these communities today reflects their past economy. They survived after the boom by becoming small regional trade and service centers for ranchers, miners and loggers. As with many other small western towns, government employment figures big in the local economy of this sparsely settled land and the U.S. Forest Service, Soil Conservation Service, Fish and Game and other state and federal agencies contribute much to the economic stability of communities like Baker, La Grande, John Day, Prineville, and Enterprise.

Headwaters of the West Fork of the Wallowa River, Eagle Cap Wilderness, Wallowa Mountains, displays the characteristic U-shaped valley of glaciated country.
GEORGE WUERTHNER

Even the climate is similar to that of the northern Rockies. The air is much drier here than it is west of the Cascades, and ski areas like Anthony Lakes are known for their dry powder. Enterprise, a typical northeast Oregon community, has summer temperatures in the 80s and seldom reaches the 90s, while winter temperatures can dip to 30 below or lower. Rainfall in the mountain valleys is rather low— Baker receives about 12" per year and Enterprise 13"— while precipitation in the mountains, which siphon away most of the moisture from passing storms, is correspondingly high and snow-depth often exceeds 10' or more.

The Blue Mountain complex stretches across nearly half the state, and encompasses many small mountain

57

Above: Sunset on Smith Rock along the Crooked River at the extreme western end of the Ochoco Mountains near Redmond. STEVE TERRILL
Right: Looking across the Crooked River and the town of Prineville to the Ochoco Mountains.
GEORGE WUERTHNER

ranges, hills and dissected plateaus from 1,500' to nearly 10,000'. Interspersed between these forested ranges are grassy basins like the upper John Day, Grande Ronde, Silvies, and Powder River valleys where most of the communities are located. Beginning near Redmond, where the cliffs at Smith Rocks State Park mark its westernmost extension, the highlands curve to the northeast in a broad arc, running out of the state where Washington and Idaho come together with Oregon. Within this region are a number of sub-ranges: to the west— the Ochoco, Maury and Aldrich mountains— and cradling the headwaters of the John Day River, the Strawberry, Greenhorn and Elkhorn mountains. These individual ranges are often collectively referred to as the Blue Mountains, but beyond La Grande and stretching into Washington is a forested plateau, dissected by deep river canyons like the Wenaha, which we'll call the Blue Mountains proper for lack of a better name.

Across the Powder River valley from the Elkhorn Mountains are the Wallowa Mountains, the highest peaks in

Oregon outside of the Cascades. A good percentage of the Wallowas are within the boundaries of the Eagle Cap Wilderness. The Wallowas are overlapped on their eastern border by lava flows that make up the deep canyons of the Imnaha and the Snake River at Hells Canyon. The high forested ridges separating these deep canyons resemble mountains, although this region is technically considered a dissected plateau.

Most of the mountains in this region were uplifted by faulting and their alignment reflects these breaks in the earth's crust. For example, the Strawberry Mountains seen from Dixie Summit appear to rise out of the John Day Valley in a rather straight east-west line, marking the fault that separates these rocks from other rocks to the north. The dramatic north side of the Wallowa Mountains seen beyond Enterprise is also the result of uplift along a northwest-trending fault. But these faults are of recent origin and to understand these mountains we must go far back in geological history— to when this region was once the edge of the continent.

A Fringe of Volcanoes

Approximately 200 million years ago, the Blue Mountain uplift was part of a mountain range that fringed a shallow ocean basin. A string of volcanoes marked the edge of a sinking ocean plate, much as the Cascades do today, and remnants of these volcanoes can still be found in the Ochoco Mountains. The volcanic andesites and basalts of the Ochocos resemble rock outcrops near Eugene, so geologists believe these two areas were once part of the same volcanic chain. The High Cascades and other later volcanic eruptions have buried the intervening rocks so that we see only the western and eastern extremities of this ancient mountain range.

After the line of volcanoes shifted to its present north-south orientation about 35 million years ago, a long period of quiet ensued. New eruptions in the western Cascades began between 25 and 30 million years ago and ash from these eruptions accumulated to depths of more than 1,000' to create what is known as the John Day formation, visible today as colorful, eroded badlands at the John Day Fossil Beds and elsewhere north of the Ochoco Mountains.

Sometime after these volcanoes stopped erupting, new ruptures opened the earth's surface in eastern Oregon and massive basalt flows poured out, covering thousands of square miles under a deluge of molten rock. These basalt plateaus are collectively known as the Columbia River Basalts. Rather than originating from one single flow, they erupted from many different sources and differ somewhat in age and composition. Flows issued from the Picture Gorge area and later from a huge volcano centered in northeast Oregon near the present-day Grande Ronde River. The Grande Ronde volcano may have been the largest volcano in the world and the extent of its flows, which cover most of northern Oregon, southern Washington, parts of Idaho and even the northern Willamette Valley, attests to the incredible amount of molten rock that poured from it.

These eruptions were not continuous, and quiet periods, sometimes hundreds of thousands of years, intervened. Soils formed on top of each new basalt layer subsequently were buried by new flows. The layers are now exposed in the soils as bright red bands of laterite (high in iron oxides) sandwiched in the darker basalts. Such soils developed under humid, tropical conditions and that Oregon was covered by lush vegetation at this time. These sandwiched lateritic soils can be seen readily in the Grande Ronde River Canyon near Troy and elsewhere.

The huge volcano centered on the Grand Ronde area completed its eruption about 12 million years ago, leaving most of northeast Oregon as a vast basalt plain from which rose only the highest peaks of the Wallowa, Ochoco and Blue mountains. River erosion later carved the canyons of the Weneha, Grande Ronde, Imnaha and Hells Canyon into these massive basalt slabs exposing the different-age flows as step-like terraces, each of slightly different hardness that weathers at its own rate.

Volcanoes also erupted in the Strawberry Mountain area. These peaks, probably similar in appearance to the present-day Cascades, produced rhyolite and andesite, and their volcanic ash drifted over much of central Oregon. The throat of one of the old volcanoes remains as a crystallized rock mass known as a plug, and is visible today as thousand-foot cliffs south of Little Strawberry Lake. Andesite lava flows from the main volcanic vent produced the bulk of the present Strawberry Mountains and appear as layers of gray rock in cliffs along the upper reaches of Strawberry Creek.

The Aldrich Mountains are formed of old seafloor sediments seen today as sandstones and shale mixed with some volcanic rocks, representing where the sea floor sank into the earth's interior, and portions were scraped off onto the continental mass. Near Canyon City along the eastern edge of these mountains, where they join the Strawberries, is a large outcrop of serpentinite. Serpentinite is formed from peridotite, a rock that is usually buried under the basalts of ocean floors and is not ordinarily found on dry land. When the ocean floor was diving under the continental plate, a piece of peridotite broke loose and attached itself to the continental crust; we see chunks of this former ocean bottom exposed as Canyon Mountain south of John Day. Placer gold deposits associated with this mineralized region were the impetus for the Canyon City gold rush in 1861.

To the east of the Strawberries the volcanic basalt flows have been eroded in places, exposing outcrops of granites. Granite forms when molten rock fails to reach the earth's surface and cools very slowly deep in the earth. Later, faulting pushes these rocks closer to the surface where erosion strips away overlying younger rocks. Because granites are very hard and resistant to erosion they create spectacular jagged peaks, particularly if they were glaciated. Many of the dramatic mountains of the West— including the Grand Tetons, the Wind River Range, Sierra Nevada, and in eastern Oregon the Wallowas, Greenhorn and Elkhorn mountains— are composed of glacially eroded granites. Pockets of mineralized rock

Junipers dot grasslands on the north slope of the Aldrich Mountains.
GEORGE WUERTHNER

Above: Strawberry Mountain, an ancient volcano, now bears a glacially carved cirque on its flanks.
GEORGE WUERTHNER
Top right: Wallowa Lake near Joseph was created when a glacial moraine blocked the Wallowa River.
STEVE TERRILL
Right: Van Patten Lake sits in a glacial valley in the Elkhorn Mountains, a popular recreation area that conservationists would like to see designated as wilderness.
GEORGE WUERTHNER

typically are associated with granites, so it is not surprising that most of Oregon's gold-rush history took place in these mountains.

The Wallowas are particularly interesting for the mix of rocks found there, including limestones, basalts and granites, which make up the bulk of the range. Pleistocene glaciers carved cirques and U-shaped valleys on the higher peaks of the Greenhorns and Elkhorns, but the Wallowas contain by far the best examples of glacial action. The lakes in the popular Lakes Basin were scooped by glaciers, and the long curving shoreline of Wallowa Lake is really a giant glacial moraine that dammed the Wallowa River. As you drive up from the town of Joseph to the lake, you cross the terminal moraine of this huge glacier.

The Elkhorns are basically a single granite ridge; numerous cirque basins on either side of the crest are dotted with small lakes, and meadows formed when shallow lakes gradually filled with sediment and were covered with vegetation. The Anthony Lakes are examples of water bodies created by glacial action. The range forms a backdrop to Baker, rising along a fault as an impressive wall of rock. This important local recreation area features the Elkhorn Crest Trail, which runs the length of these mountains.

Glaciers also carved cirques and lakes in the Strawberry Mountains. Strawberry Lake is a moraine-dammed lake like the larger Wallowa Lake. Unglaciated valleys and mountains such as those in the Ochocos country and the Blue Mountain plateau, drained by the Wenah, Umatilla and Grande Ronde rivers have gentler relief than glaciated terrain, except where rivers have cut deep V-shaped canyons.

Mining Country

Because of the extensive outcrops of granite, which often bear mineralized pockets, the area experienced some of the heaviest prospecting and mining activity in the entire state. Gold was discovered in 1862 by five former Confederate soldiers, on the Powder River near the present-day site of Sumpter. They named the town for Fort Sumter (later changed to Sumpter) in South Carolina, where the Civil War began. At first only placer gold was recovered from the river gravels, but later gold-bearing veins were discovered in the surrounding mountains, giving further impetus to development of the region. By 1903 the town numbered 500 people and boasted 15 saloons and two newspapers. In 1917 a fire nearly leveled the town and the populace began to drift away.

Just outside Sumpter rests a gold dredge, looking like a beached whale. The dredge began operating on the Powder River in 1913 and was used on and off until 1954. A dredge digs up stream gravels with its giant shovel and washes out the placer gold, spilling excess gravel in piles behind it, as it slowly crawls up a valley. The Sumpter dredge produced more gold than any other placer operation in the state. Between 1946 and 1954 it produced more gold than all the other placer and lode operations combined.

The Sumpter Valley Railroad, which began operation in 1891, was built primarily to haul logs from the mountains to mills in Baker, but by 1896 the line had reached Sumpter and began to haul ore also. Spur lines were built to Prairie City to carry cattle and supplies to ranchers in the upper John Day country. The railroad was abandoned in 1947. Today the little narrow-gauge railroad has been reactivated and visitors can ride a replica of the old steam engine up the Powder River valley.

Almost nothing remains of Auburn, located southwest of Baker, although it was once the largest town in Oregon, serving as a supply center for the gold fields in the surrounding mountains. Within one year of the 1862 gold strike more than 5,000 people called Auburn home. Supplies came to the town by pack train and prices were

high. Flour sold for $28 per hundred pounds; bacon was 50¢ a pound; and eggs were 25¢ each. Auburn was short-lived and once the estimated $10 million in gold had been taken from the placers, the county seat was moved to Baker and Auburn collapsed.

Several miners on their way to Auburn in 1862 camped for the evening on a tributary of the John Day River. One of these men, William Allard, found gold in the creek the following morning as they were breaking camp. This began the rush to Canyon City. These placer deposits, with an estimated take of $26,000,000, were the richest placer discoveries in Oregon. A single panning of these gravels could sometimes reap $150 in gold! As in much of Oregon, the Canyon City gold fields had a substantial population of Chinese miners who, according to Oregon law, were not allowed to hold real estate or work any mining claim themselves. Many Chinese were forced to hire white men who would hold the claim in name, and receive a cut of the profits, while the Orientals did all the work. In the 1880s the laws were relaxed somewhat and the Chinese were allowed to own mining claims. Many reworked the ground abandoned by white miners and because of their diligence, were able to amass sizeable fortunes.

Sumpter as it looked around the turn of the century when it was one of the major gold-mining communities in the Blue Mountains.
OREGON HISTORICAL SOCIETY PHOTO

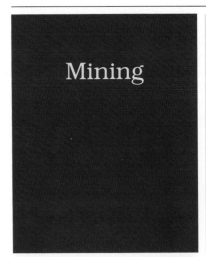

Mining

Above: Abandoned gold dredge at Sumpter.
Right: People still search the gravels of the Blue Mountains for gold, as here along the North Fork of the John Day.
GEORGE WUERTHNER PHOTOS

Valuable minerals such as gold, silver and copper are found in minute amounts over most of the earth, but mining is feasible only in a few places, where concentration has occurred. Oxygen is an abundant element comprising 46.60 percent by weight of the earth's crust, while other elements such as copper (.007 percent) are much more scarce. Gold (.0000005 percent) is one of the least abundant and to find gold in a concentrated form is extremely rare. Mineralization occurs deep in the earth under heat and pressure as rising magma, in combination with water, dissolves the widely dispersed scarce minerals like gold and concentrates them in solution. The ascending magma forces itself into cracks or weak structural areas of the already existing rock, called country rock, and cooks it. The magma and its attendant super-heated mineralized water eventually cool and elements such as gold are precipitated out to form veins and lode deposits.

Gold and other valuable minerals are frequently found in association with granite batholiths or stocks. Most of the Cascade Range, which is primarily extruded volcanic rocks, is poor in valuable minerals. Thus few rushed for gold to this portion of the state. The occasional gold discoveries, like Bohemia, Quartzville, Blue River and others, are connected with granitic intrusions into the otherwise unmineralized basalts and other volcanic rocks. The major gold rush regions of the state are concentrated in the older rocks found in the Siskiyou and Blue mountain sub-ranges, like the Elkhorns and Greenhorns, where erosion has exposed gold-bearing veins near the surface.

In Oregon, gold was found in both placer and lode deposits. Lodes are ledges of concentrated, mineralized rock buried in the ground as veins. Mining lodes requires a great deal of effort and usually machinery to tunnel into the mountainside, break the ore-bearing rock into manageable chunks, and finally separate the valuable mineral from its associated country rock. The rubble is discarded as tailings. Miners follow veins deep into the mountains hoping to find a "pocket," or area of higher concentration. Because of the expense involved in this kind of mining, it usually requires the formation of a company with miners working for wages.

The lonely, wandering prospector with whom most of us associate the gold rush days was usually in search of placer or stream-deposited gold. Gold-bearing rock is eroded from an exposed lode deposit and washed into a stream, where water pounds and pulverizes the ore for

centuries and eventually frees the gold, mixing it with sand and gravel. Placer mining involves washing away these gravels and extracting the gold, a relatively simple process. The requisite equipment—a gold pan or sluice box—was cheap and easily obtained and hence placer mining was the most common and dispersed form of gold mining.

Panning, sluicing and dredging are all versions of the same process, that of separating the gold from the gravels. Because gold is heavier than nearly all other elements, it eventually becomes trapped behind bedrock ledges and large boulders. To work a placer deposit, miners dug up stream-deposited gravels either from an existing riverbed, or from ancient river terraces, then washed away rocks and sand with water in a gold pan or sent the water flowing over small riffles in a sluicebox. The precious mineral was left behind.

A gold dredge can be thought of as a larger version of a sluice box. A giant shovel scoops gravels and rocks from a river, then runs them over a conveyor belt that sorts the material, spitting out the tailings and concentrating the gold-bearing gravels that are then worked by a smaller sluice box, or are panned, to remove the gold. All placer mining has a negative impact on streambank stability and water quality, but dredging operations have literally rearranged entire valleys and left behind barren landscapes of unsorted rock like those in the Powder River valley by Sumpter.

Theoretically, the concentration of placer gold in a streambed should increase as one gets closer to the lode deposit from which the gold was originally eroded. Many placer miners panned their way upstream hoping to discover the bedrock source or "mother lode."

The gold in lode deposits often was mixed with other materials and had to be separated. The ore was crushed first. One of the earliest means of crushing gold-bearing ore was the arrastra, which was used extensively in remote mines of Mexico. The arrastra was just a large stone dragged around a circular bed by animals or by water power, grinding the ore much like an old-fashioned flour mill.

The next step up in efficiency was the stamp mill, which crushed more ore, faster. Like the pistons in a car engine, the stamp mill lifted heavy pestles up and down, pulverizing the ore that passed beneath them. Stamp mills were more costly to operate, and were usually associated only with the larger mines.

Once the ore was crushed, the gold still had to be separated from the pulverized rock. One method involved coating a copper table with mercury— which has a strong affinity for gold— and passing the crushed ore over it. The gold later was separated from the mercury.

Another method frequently used to remove gold from its overburden was the flotation process. The ore was added to a frothing mixture, which caused the gold to float to the surface where it was skimmed off.

No matter which method of mining was used, most of the high grade, concentrated and easily accessible gold has been found and recovered. There is still plenty of gold in "them thar" hills, but at such low concentrations and grades that more expense and energy would go into extraction than the mineral presently is worth. If the price of gold rises significantly, however, people will once again scour the hills, seeking their fortunes among the rocks.

Abandoned miner's cabin within the North Fork of the John Day Wilderness is a reminder of the region's frontier past.
GEORGE WUERTHNER

The Greenhorn Mountains form a drainage divide between the Burnt River and the John Day, and were also an early gold mining region. The mountains are named for an outcrop of green serpentine rock that early travelers used as a landmark. The town of Greenhorn sprang up in 1891 after gold was discovered in the nearby mountains. The townsite, with numerous saloons, was 14 acres in size. This posed a problem for the local school, which by Oregon law could not be within a quarter mile of any drinking establishment. To resolve the problem, the city petitioned the President of the United States for a land grant to expand the town's borders. The request was granted by President Taft, making it the only community in the country with a patent to its townsite obtained by executive order.

At one time about 2,000 people received mail at Greenhorn and in winter early mail carriers skied to the town over the deep snow cloaking the area. Eventually the mines closed and by 1919 the town was virtually deserted. Like many other ghost towns, Greenhorn has seen a resurgence of interest as people seek out summer homes in the mountains. It has the distinction of being Oregon's highest (6,271') and smallest incorporated town (six housing units, no year-round residents in 1980 census).

Jagged Peaks and Wilderness

For a close look at the Elkhorns and Greenhorns, one should take the Elkhorn Drive, which passes through the Anthony Lakes area, the old gold mining districts of Granite and Sumpter, and through the Powder River

63

Valley. One will also pass dozens of clearcuts where the Forest Service attempted to eradicate pine beetles from overstocked lodgepole stands.

The highest and most dramatic peaks in this sub-region are found in the Wallowa Mountains and contain some of the most continuous subalpine country found in Oregon. Among the higher peaks are Matterhorn (9,832'), Petes Peak (9,675'), Aneroid Mountain (9,702'), Sacajawea Peak (9,839'), Red Mountain (9,555'), Chief Joseph (9,617') and Eagle Cap (9,595'). More than 60 lakes are found in these mountains and Legore Lake at 8,880' is reputed to be the highest lake in Oregon, excluding a tiny pond above 10,000' in the crater of South Sister.

Most of the mountain range is part of the 361,446-acre Eagle Cap Wilderness, the largest wilderness area in Oregon. The area is approximately 20 miles by 20 miles in size, and yet only a small portion gets most of the use due to a geographical fluke. The major river valleys of the Wallowas are arranged like spokes of a wheel and radiate from Eagle Cap Peak. Nearly all the drainages, such as the Lostine, Minam, Eagle Creek, Imnaha and Wallowa, have trails along their courses, and all lead to the central lake-studded basin below Eagle Cap Peak, which sometimes causes overcrowding.

Many people consider the Wallowas to be the most beautiful mountain range in Oregon and local boosters like to refer to it as the "Switzerland of America." The scenery was immortalized in the movie *Paint Your Wagon*, which was filmed on Eagle Creek in the Wallowas and by Anthony Lakes in the Elkhorns.

Cornucopia, on the southern edge of the range, was a center of mining activity until recently. One mine produced more than 75,000 ounces of gold, 350,000 ounces of silver and 350,000 pounds of copper. In the early 1900s hard-rock mining employed 700 men at the site, but during World War II the federal government closed all non-essential mining, and Cornucopia's period of productivity came to an end. Today many of the old buildings and cabins are summer homes.

The forest vegetation throughout all these ranges is remarkably similar, and not as diverse as in the Cascades or Siskiyous. On the fringes of grasslands one finds the western juniper growing in scattered savannas, particularly on the drier, low-elevation slopes in the western Blue Mountain Ranges such as the Ochoco and Aldrich mountains. Open stands of ponderosa pine dominate this region and more than half the ponderosa pine on the Malheur National Forest are old, large-

diameter trees, making it perhaps the largest stand of old-growth ponderosa pine in the world. However, the Malheur Forest Service district is rapidly liquidating these mature stands, and this claim may soon be a thing of the past.

Lodgepole pine grows in the moister areas, particularly in the headwaters of the North Fork John Day, Powder and Grande Ronde rivers. Extensive, overcrowded stands of this tree have been naturally thinned by pine beetles who kill the less vigorous individuals and thus improve the growth and productivity of the survivors. Once a stand has been thinned, the resulting forest is no longer suitable for pine beetle and the outbreak dies out. Grand fir and Douglas fir, western larch, and Engelmann spruce are abundant species, while western white pine is present in limited numbers.

At high elevations are subalpine fir, white bark pine, and in the Wallowas, mountain hemlock and limber pine. Limber pine is a common species in the Rockies and Great Basin, but the Wallowas are the only place in

Left: Eagle Cap Peak from a tarn near Horton Pass. Wallowa Mountains.
LARRY ULRICH
Above: Evening along West Fork Wallowa River in the Eagle Cap Wilderness, Wallowa Mountains.
GEORGE WUERTHNER

Facing page: Jagged peaks in the Eagle Cap Wilderness, part of the Wallowa Mountains. PAT O'HARA

Clumps of bluebunch wheatgrass grow on a slope above the Wenaha River Canyon in the Wenaha-Tuccannon Wilderness in the Blue Mountains where it straddles the Oregon-Washington border.
GEORGE WUERTHNER

other towns in the late 1800s, shipment of lumber to markets outside the local area became possible and logging became a major activity. Old-growth ponderosa pine was the major species harvested, and logging often occurred in the winter when trees could be skidded over the snow. The logs were dragged to the nearest river; in June when the water was highest, they were floated to the mill. At times the loggers constructed "splash dams," which were dynamited to release a surge of water to move the logs down the river.

Beautiful grasslands containing bluebunch wheatgrass and Idaho fescue cloak many of the lower canyons and slopes of these mountains. Open parks and grasslands are more common here than in the Cascades and were grazed by domestic sheep herds. The area was particularly attractive because the sheep could be wintered in the low elevation canyons like the Imnaha and Hells canyons, then driven to lush summer meadows in places like the Wallowas. Near the turn of the century as many as 380,000 sheep were grazed in the Wallowa Mountains within what is now the Eagle Cap Wilderness. An early photographer of the Wallowas made this comment about the condition of the sheep ranges: "...the grass has been nearly destroyed by early grazing. The snow is hardly gone, but the sheep have made mud of the hills." The heavy grazing caused severe damage to the grasslands, especially at high elevations, and they have not yet recovered. Many of the mountain meadows I visited in the Elkhorns and Wallowas still had a very limited plant cover of only a few species as a result of the excessive grazing they suffered nearly a century ago. Ironically, many of these areas are still grazed, although with considerably fewer animals and for shorter periods of time.

In 1902 a four-year range war erupted between sheepmen and cattlemen. Beginning in the 1860s stockmen began to infiltrate the Blue Mountain region to take advantage of the lush native grasslands. Both sheep and cattle were moved from home ranches each spring to mountain pastures, which at this time were "open range" and available to whoever got there first and was strong enough to keep it. Competition was keen for grasses, and it was inevitable that conflict would result.

During the range war, a group of cattlemen from the Ochocos organized themselves into the Crook County Sheep Shooters Association and, vowed to secrecy, began to terrorize sheep herders and their flocks. Methodically, this group rode into sheep camps, bound and blindfolded the herders, and shot all the sheep they could find. One group of 11 masked association mem-

Oregon where this tree is found. A relict population of Alaskan yellow cedar grows in the Aldrich Mountains, the only place in Oregon east of the Cascades where it is seen. Scattered throughout these mountains are stands of aspen, adding a touch of gold to the otherwise somber greens each autumn. One small patch of paper birch, a species common farther north in Canada, is found along the Minam River.

Logging, Grazing and Overuse Too

Logging of these forests began shortly after the first gold rushes when timber was needed to build the towns and mine structures. After the railroads reached Baker and

bers killed 2,400 sheep in one raid near Benjamin Lake south of the Maury Mountains and in 1904 more than 1,000 sheep were killed at Little Summit Prairie in the Ochocos. Other herders suffered similar losses. In addition to direct killings, flocks were spooked and scattered, hay fields were burned and threats were made to anyone who raised sheep or cooperated with sheep raisers in any manner. This free-enterprise system was finally brought to an end when the newly established national forests began a system of grazing permits that allotted pastures to individual ranchers.

Elk, Deer, Lions, Bears

Although competition with livestock limited the recovery of some wildlife species such as bighorn sheep, others like elk have rebounded from turn-of-the-century lows. The elk population of the Wallowa-Whitman National Forest is the largest found on any national forest in the country, and altogether northeast Oregon is home to more than 53,000 elk according to 1986 estimates. Elk outnumber residents in Wallowa County three to one. Yet it was not always this way. Elk season was closed from 1899 until 1904 because the elk population was so low due to overhunting and competition from domestic livestock. The season was closed again in 1908, and in 1912 15 elk trapped in Jackson Hole, Wyoming were transported to Wallowa county and released. A second transplant of 15 more elk occurred the following year and in 1933 the elk season opened again.

Unfortunately, the region's famed elk hunting is declining as a result of the continuously expanding forest road system, which fragments elk security cover and increases general harassment. There are 9,300 miles of roads on the Wallowa-Whitman Forest, 7,200 on the Malheur Forest, 4,500 on the Ochoco, and yet new roads are being constructed. The elk herds are huge, but so is the number killed each year due to easy access.

Except for small numbers of whitetail deer in bottom lands along the Snake River, mule deer are the only deer species found in the entire region and they numbered 165,750 in 1986. This number is considered low because of successive hard winters. Elk and mule deer are migratory, spending their winters in the low elevations and moving with the advance of spring up the mountains into the high meadows and basins.

The elk and deer help sustain the largest mountain lion populations in the state, and lions are particularly abundant in the Eagle Cap Wilderness area. Black bear, another predator, is found throughout the region, as was

the grizzly until it was extirpated. The last known grizzly sighting in the state occurred in Wallowa County in 1931. A grizzly was reported in the Hells Canyon area in 1984, and it's possible an individual wandered over from Idaho, but more likely a cinnamon-colored black bear was seen, since this color phase is common in the Hells Canyon region.

Bighorn sheep were once common in the Blue Mountain region, but overhunting combined with grazing competition from domestic livestock eliminated these herds. Sheep were recently replanted in several areas and they now number approximately 400 head, with 120 in the Wallowas and smaller herds scattered elsewhere. Transplants were made recently to Canyon Mountain and the Aldrich Mountains by John Day, Strawberry Mountains, Imnaha River, Lostine River, Hells Canyon and elsewhere. One planting of nine sheep captured in the Wallo- and released around Troy on the Grande Ronde River failed because the sheep wandered the 50 miles back to their home range in the Eagle Cap Wilderness.

Most biologists agree that mountain goats were never native to the area, or if they were, hunting eliminated them early, for no credible record exists for this species. Goats were transplanted to the Eagle Cap Wilderness in the 1950s, but they have not prospered. The herd numbers about 35 to 40 and remains static. Biologists believe that genetic inbreeding may be the problem and in 1985 nine more goats were transplanted to the herd to alleviate this problem. Goats also were released recently in the Elkhorn Mountains and the herd now numbers between 15 and 20.

Antelope are found in the upper John Day valley and on the south side of the Strawberry and Aldrich mountains in the upper Silvies Valley. Antelope tend to avoid forested areas, but will pass through on migrations.

All the higher mountains such as the Strawberrys, Elkhorns and Wallowas have the small rabbit-like creature, the pika. Furbearers such as weasel, marten, and wolverine are found, but wolverines are exceedingly rare. The fisher, once extinct, was successfully reestablished in the Eagle Cap Wilderness in 1961. Beaver, another important furbearer, is abundant and has recovered from the depletion of the fur trapping era.

More than 269 bird species have been reported for Union and Wallowa counties alone, and it is likely that at least 300 species could be found throughout this entire region. In the forested areas lives the goshawk, an accipiter (the hawk family) that hunts snowshoe rabbits, grouse and

Sheep grazing near Enterprise beneath the Wallowa Mountains.
GEORGE WUERTHNER

A ranch on the rolling uplands above the Grande Ronde River near Flora.
GEORGE WUERTHNER

white and black birds, approximately the size of crows, use their stout bill to chisel 2" to 4" rectangular holes in trees, where they seek beetles and other insects, their main food.

In alpine areas of the Wallowa Mountains, one might see the Wallowa gray crowned rosy finch, found nowhere else in the world. This bird breeds only above timberline, feeding on insects it finds on snowfields. The white-tailed ptarmigan, a small grouse inhabiting alpine areas, was introduced into the Eagle Cap in 1967, but is exceedingly rare. It turns pure white in winter, but is a mottled brown color in summer.

There are seven river systems in northeast Oregon, all of which at one time supported anadromous fish runs. The Hells Canyon dam destroyed anadromous runs on the Burnt and Powder rivers, and the Grande Ronde, Walla-Walla and Imnaha have vestiges of wild fisheries supplemented by hatchery releases. Salmon runs were extinct on the Umatilla for 60 years and were only recently re-established with marginal success. Only the John Day River supports a completely wild fishery and it seems to be recovering from many years of marginal runs. In 1986 this river had outstanding runs of 3,000 salmon and nearly 30,000 steelhead.

All these rivers suffer from a variety of problems including barriers to migration such as dams on the lower Columbia, water draw-downs for irrigation, and riparian zone damage from grazing, which destabilizes banks and results in shallower and wider streams. Sedimentation from logging roads is also a problem.

These fisheries once supported small groups of Indians who lived scattered throughout the river valleys, supplementing their fish diet with roots, berries, and wild game such as elk and deer. Once the horse reached these people in the early 1700s, the entire mode of subsistence changed for some tribes. Populations increased, and because tribes could gather resources from much wider areas, individual villages could be larger. With horses they could cross the mountains and hunt bison in Montana. Despite this new source of food many tribes still relied upon salmon runs for a good part of their diet, and when runs were poor, many people starved. Lewis and Clark on their eastward trek mention that the Nez Perce were recovering from a hard winter in which hunger was rampant. "We are informed that the natives in this quarter were much distressed for food last winter and were compelled to collect the moss which grows on the pine, which they boiled and ate."

other animals. The goshawk is particularly aggressive around its nest and will not hesitate to swoop down on any interloper. I was attacked numerous times by a pair I encountered in a dense larch-lodgepole forest in the Wallowa Mountains. With their red eyes, these birds are fierce looking, especially when they are diving for your head! Fortunately, most of these displays are bluffs and if you leave the area, the birds are content to leave you alone.

Another relatively rare bird of prey is the great gray owl, the largest owl in Oregon. It typically inhabits higher-elevation forests broken by occasional meadows and openings. A species dependent on old-growth forests, snags and cavities is the pileated woodpecker. These red,

Wilderness and Wilderness That Could Be

Little of the lands occupied by the Indians still appears as it did 150 years ago, but a few mountainous areas are now designated wilderness. As mentioned, the Eagle Cap Wilderness is Oregon's largest. With the passage of the 1984 Oregon wilderness bill several areas including the Strawberry Mountains and Wenaha-Tucannon were enlarged, and the Mill Creek, Bridge Creek, Black Canyon, Monument Peak and North Fork of the Umatilla areas were legally designated as wilderness.

A 400,000-acre wilderness was proposed for the North Fork of the John Day, but only 121,800 acres were designated in the 1984 bill. Logging is rapidly whittling away at the remaining non-designated roadless country, and since 1984 more than 75,000 acres of the original 400,000 have been roaded and harvested.

A controversial proposal to log extensive areas of the 660,000-acre Hells Canyon National Recreation Area has sparked a new debate about the merits of more wilderness designation for this highly scenic canyon that straddles the Idaho and Oregon border. One of the attractions of the NRA is the 6,982' gorge carved by the Snake River through the basalt flows laid down by the old Grande Ronde volcano. One of the best views in the west can be seen from the Hat Point overlook, accessible by car, which gives a superb panorama of Hells Canyon, the deepest gorge in North America, as well as a view of the Seven Devils Mountains across the river in Idaho.

Although 213,993 acres are now designated wilderness, conservationists are proposing that another 300,000 acres of the Hells Canyon area be designated wilderness in an effort to keep it oriented toward recreation. Imaginative conservationists have endorsed a proposal based on biology rather than political boundaries, designed to protect an entire ecosystem from river bottoms to alpine peaks, by combining the Eagle Cap Wilderness with the Hells Canyon NRA. A few dirt roads in the upper Imnaha and Lake Fork drainages would be closed and the landscape would be allowed to revert to a nearly pristine condition. If the two areas were linked and all present roadless country were excluded from timber harvest, it would preserve a million or more acres of undisturbed wildlife habitat, making it Oregon's greatest wildland and biological preserve.

The Rockies may seem distant to people living in the Willamette Valley, but for many northeast Oregon residents living among the peaks and basins of the Blue Mountains, they are only a step away from their back doors.

Left: The Snake River flowing through Hells Canyon, as seen from Hat Point. The abundance of low-elevation big-game winter range along river canyons like this helps support one of the largest elk herds in the nation.

Below: Imnaha River Canyon, part of the Hells Canyon National Recreation Area.
GEORGE WUERTHNER PHOTOS

CHAPTER 8

The Siskiyous

Above: Jeffrey pine cones amid wildflowers on a serpentine soil site by Cave Junction.

Right: Sitka spruce frames golden hills that plunge into the sea at Samuel Broadman State Park north of Brookings.
GEORGE WUERTHNER PHOTOS

The Siskiyous, part of the Klamath Mountains, are a bit of California that laps over into Oregon. These peaks and valleys fill the southwest corner of the state from the Pacific Ocean to the Cascades, and it is generally agreed that the Siskiyous' northern boundary is located along the Middle Fork of the Coquille River while the southern end of the range extends into northern California. The greatest elevations are found in the eastern portion of the range in the headwaters of the Applegate River and Bear Creek where Mount Ashland (7,530') is the highest summit. Other high peaks include Dutchman Peak (7,418'), Grayback Mountain (7,055') and Lake Peak (6,642'). Although the summits are not high in an absolute sense, they rise from the low valleys as much as 5,000'.

The Golden State traveler is immediately at ease in this part of Oregon. Unlike the northern Coast Range with its heavily timbered slopes rushing headlong into the sea, the coastal edge of the Siskiyous is reminiscent of California's Big Sur coastline, having emerald grassy hills (amber in late summer) interspersed with forested gullies and complete with Oregon's only redwoods. Around Medford on the eastern slopes of the Siskiyous, where a sunny Mediterranean climate dominates a landscape of oak savannas interspersed with vineyards and wineries, it is easy to imagine oneself in the wine country of Sonoma County north of San Francisco. Jacksonville, a former gold rush town, emulates in architecture and setting communities in the Sierra Mother Lode country.

The resemblance does not end with the look of the land, for California visitors regularly flood this part of Oregon and make up by far the greatest percentage of out-of-state tourists. Some would say that southwest Oregon has become a colony of California as migrants from the giant to the south buy cut-over "stump ranches" to take advantage of the region's relatively benign climate and uncrowded spaces or retire more luxuriously in communities like Grants Pass, Ashland and Medford.

California Invades Oregon

The Siskiyous are a geological and geographical extension of a California mountain region with many subranges, all covered by a blanket term, the Klamath Mountains. These geologically-old highlands are deeply dissected by rivers with steep-walled canyons. They appear from any high peak as an endless series of ridges merging into a thin blue line at the far horizon. Despite their overall low elevation, subalpine meadowlands abound, and grassy, open ridgelines give these mountains an alpine appearance.

Ranch along the Applegate River.
GEORGE WUERTHNER

The Siskiyous are the oldest exposed rocks in Oregon and were once part of a coastal mountain range that included the Sierras. These mountains were formed about 200 million years ago when the North American continent began to break apart from Europe. As it moved westward, the floor of the Pacific Ocean slid under the continental plate, shoving sediments on the coastal plain and continental shelf against the western edge of the plate. The oldest rocks are those to the east, while the most recent are exposed along the western edge of the range.

One visible remnant of old sea floor sediments can be seen at Oregon Caves National Monument east of Cave Junction. The caves are formed in 200-million-year-old rocks that were deposited on the ocean floor and compacted into limestone. Heat and pressure restructured the limestone into marble, and weak acids found naturally in rainwater dissolved some of the rock to create the caves we find today.

Occasionally a portion of the seafloor itself was broken off and mixed in with the growing pile of scrambled

71

Left to right: Thin cover of Jeffrey pine on an outcrop of nutrient-poor serpentine soils along the Illinois River.
Manzanita and mountain mahogany near timberline on Dutchman's Peak near the headwaters of the Applegate River.
Only the highest peaks of the Siskiyous experienced glaciation. Seen here are the still waters of the glacially-carved Babyfoot Lake in the Kalmiopsis Wilderness.
GEORGE WUERTHNER PHOTOS

rocks. These are exposed as serpentine outcrops throughout the Kalmiopsis Wilderness. The greenish serpentine has a shiny, greasy look and is easily squeezed into fractures in the earth's crust, which is why outcrops usually mark fault zones. Soils derived from this rock are high in iron, chrome, cobalt and nickel. Commercial extraction of nickel occurs near the town of Riddle, although the profitability of the mine varies with the price of the mineral and in recent years the mine has operated sporadically. Soils in the Illinois Valley and by Gold Beach are potential sites for new nickel mining operations as long as nickel prices are high.

Some of the rocks in the Siskiyous were formed by magma that melted and worked its way toward the surface to erupt as volcanoes, but most have long since eroded away. In places the molten rock failed to reach the surface and cooled to form granites. Erosion has since stripped away the overlying rock, and these hard granitic outcrops appear on Mount Ashland, the headwaters of the Applegate River and elsewhere in the range.

Between 150 and 100 million years ago, the Sisikyous and the rest of the Klamath Mountains to the south broke away from the coastal mountain chain and slid westward to become a coastal island. Fossil sea shells 100 million years of age are now found on the eastern flank of these mountains near Medford, but by 50 million years ago the sea had disappeared from this region and these mountains were once again part of the mainland.

Since that time few new materials have been added to the region, and erosion has stripped away many of the older deposits. Changes in the appearance of the land have mostly resulted from erosional processes rather than from new mountain building events. Glaciation was not widespread in these mountains, but the highest peaks do bear glacial cirques. In addition, during the glacial period when rainfall was more plentiful than at present, many rivers such as the Rogue and Illinois increased their erosive power to create the deep river canyons seen today. The branching pattern of watersheds was established as the rivers cut down into what was essentially an uplifted peneplain, or vast plain smoothed by erosion.

Annual precipitation has no doubt declined since glacial times, but depending on where you are in these mountains the amount of rainfall can still be significant. Brookings, a coastal town, receives 13" of rain during the month of January alone. Some of the ocean-facing mountains receive more than 120" of precipitation a year—almost 11' of water! Yet the interior valley communities such as Grants Pass and Medford, lying in the rain shadow of the mountains farther west, are relatively dry for western Oregon. Grants Pass has an annual precipitation average of 32.7" a year, while Medford receives even less per annum— 17". As in the rest of western Oregon, the precipitation is concentrated in the winter months: An average of 27.88" falls on Grants Pass between the months of September and March with 5.8" occurring in January alone, but less than .25" falls in July.

As might be expected, coastal communities have relatively mild weather year-round, while temperature extremes are greater in interior valleys than in the rest of western Oregon. Grants Pass has a record high of 110 degrees and a low of minus one. Heat waves reaching 100 degrees or more are relatively common in the summer months and the hot temperatures combined with the typically dry weather stress plants and animals.

The wet, mild winters and the dry, hot summers, acting in concert with the great geological, topographical and altitudinal diversity of the Siskiyous, have contributed to the development of Oregon's most diverse and richest flora. The lack of intense glacial activity made these mountains a refugium during the Ice Age, another reason for the exotic mix of plant species. Plants typical of the California Sierras, the Oregon Cascades and the Coast Ranges, are mixed with many endemic species in this one region. South-facing low-elevation slopes are covered with chaparral, and at other low-elevation sites one can find tan oak, chinquapin, black oak, and madrone. On the higher slopes are such characteristically Sierran tree species as incense cedar, Jeffrey pine, sugar pine, and Shasta red fir.

The coastal fog belt near Brookings supports small relict stands of coast redwood, a species restricted to California except for these groves in the extreme southwest corner of Oregon. Species common to the Coast Range farther north include western hemlock, Sitka spruce and the coastal form of lodgepole pine.

The major east-west orientation of the Siskiyous allows them to act as a natural corridor for species moving between the coast and the Cascades. Plants with Cascade affinities include western white pine, silver fir, and Alaska yellow cedar, while Brewer's spruce and Port Orford cedar are two species endemic to the region. Other tree species such as Douglas fir, mountain hemlock, and white fir, relatively common in their respective habitats throughout Oregon, are also found here.

Above: White oak savanna near Medford.

Left: Sugar pine, a tree typical of California's Sierra Nevada, near the Kalmiopsis Wilderness. The Siskyous are a crossroads for regional plants, and have the most diverse flora in the state.
GEORGE WUERTHNER PHOTOS

Siskiyou Specialties: Serpentine Soils, Rare Plants

The special serpentine soils are abundantly scattered throughout the region, their rock belts sparsely vegetated because of too many or too few critical elements. Non-serpentine soils may be cloaked in dense forest, while adjacent swaths of serpentine soil are dotted with a few trees as if the slope had been selectively logged. Stunted forests of Jeffrey pine, a California species, with its understory of grasses and an occasional shrub such as white-leaved manzanita comprise the only plant growth on these serpentine areas in the lower elevations. At higher altitudes the tree cover usually includes knob-cone pine, Jeffrey pine, Douglas fir, sugar pine, and incense cedar. Travelers can look for a large outcrop of serpentine soil just south of Cave Junction along Highway 199, made noticeable by the shrubby open pine forests along both sides of the road.

Many rare or endangered plant species are unique to the Siskiyous, and in 1982 the Siskiyou National Forest listed 87 sensitive species, many of which are also restricted to serpentine soils. One site, Eight Dollar Mountain along the Illinois River, has 28 sensitive species including the insect-eating pitcher plant, *Darlingtonia*, as well as California lady's slipper, Siskiyou butterweed, western violet, Siskiyou fritillaria, Howell's mariposa lily, Waldo gentian, and silky balsamroot. These plants are not likely to be on most people's list of familiar species, but they are nevertheless an important part of the region's botanical treasure. The Kalmiopsis Wilderness is named for a rare shrub, the *Kalmiopsis leachiana*, which is restricted to moist areas in these mountains.

Other oddities in tree distribution include very small patches of sub-alpine fir and aspen on Mount Ashland, a stand of lodgepole pine along Tamarack Creek, and a relict population of Engelmann spruce along the east fork of Ashland Creek. Some of the southernmost stands of Alaska yellow cedar occur on Mount Emily and in the headwaters of the Applegate River, and the northernmost stands of Baker's cypress are found near Miller Lake and Steve's Peak.

One of the Siskiyous' most beautiful trees is the lacy and graceful Brewer's spruce. Sometimes called the weeping spruce for its long, drooping branchlets, the Brewer's spruce is found nowhere else in the world except for isolated populations in southwest Oregon and northern California. This relict species once had a much wider distribution, but today is mostly confined to north-facing rocky slopes where the likelihood of fire is minimal. It is thought that the flexible branches help it to shed snow

in the heavy snowfall regions it typically occupies. The tree grows on sites with low soil fertility and little direct sunlight, but it appears to be restricted to these areas not from preference, but as a result of competition from more aggressive species that dominate the better sites.

Another tree limited in range to the Siskiyous and northern California is the Port Orford cedar, named for the small coastal town where the first lumbering of this species occurred. The tree was once a popular ornamental and has been widely planted around the world. It is restricted to wet, boggy drainages and riparian areas along the coast and appears to do well wherever soils are saturated for much of the growing season. The best stands were found on the foothills and marine terraces from Coos Bay south to Port Orford and giant old-growth forests with trees 8' to 10' in diameter once were common.

Although the old-growth cedar forests are being logged at a rapid rate, a new threat poses the possibility of extinction for the species. A root rot, first noticed in 1923 among nursery plantings, was originally confined to cultivated trees, but sometime in the early 1950s the fungus escaped to wild populations and began to destroy the species throughout its natural range.

Ironically, it is not the logging of the trees that directly threatens the species but the associated road construction and road maintenance that quickly distributes the spores to new drainages. No cure for the disease is known, and extinction may be only a matter of time. The root rot spreads in mud in the treads of logging trucks and other machinery and in mud clinging to the hooves of cattle and elk.

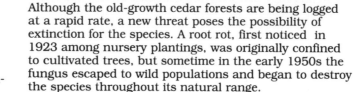

Top left: Humbug Mountain, 1,748', rises dramatically from the sea south of Port Orford. Top right: Serpentine rock has a green, greasy appearance. Above: Brewer's spruce, sometimes called weeping spruce, is endemic to the Siskiyous and adjacent parts of southern Oregon and northern California. Facing page: Granite boulders on Mt. Ashland frame the Siskiyous along the California border. GEORGE WUERTHNER PHOTOS

Deep river canyons and steep slopes characterize the Siskiyous, as here at sunset by the Chetco River drainage in the Kalmiopsis Wilderness, which would be incorporated into the proposed Siskiyou National Park. GEORGE WUERTHNER

positive influence on these forests and the Forest Service is changing its policies to include some limited "prescribed burns."

The first Europeans traveling the region were after furs. In February of 1827 a Hudson's Bay Company fur brigade led by Peter Skene Ogden became the first whites to penetrate the region. Ogden traversed the Siskiyou Crest and followed the Applegate River, eventually hitting the Rogue River, which he also explored before heading north to the Willamette Valley and Fort Vancouver.

Another Hudson's Bay Company trapping party crossing the mountains a year later lost horses near the crest. One of the French Canadian mixed-bloods who spoke the Cree Indian dialect, named the mountains Siskiyou, which was a Cree word for pack horse. Other trappers entering the region included the American, Jedediah Smith, who in 1828 led the first overland expedition from California into Oregon. His party was attacked by Indians just north of the Siskiyous along the Umpqua River and 15 of his men were killed. Smith and three others survived and sought help from the Hudson's Bay Company post at Fort Vancouver. Chief factor John McLoughlin aided his American competitors by sending a brigade south with Smith to investigate the incident and to help Smith recover some of his furs and horses.

The First Siskiyouans

The local Indian groups included the Shastas, Shasta-Costa, Chetco, Takelma, Dakubetede and others. Some of the tribes had been in the region for hundreds of years, while others such as the Mollala, who roamed the upper Rogue country just north of Medford, arrived in the region around 1750 A.D.— only 50 years before Lewis and Clark entered Oregon from the east. All these bands relied on fish, salmon and steelhead as the mainstays of their diet, while elk, deer, bear and other big game supplemented their food supplies. On the coast, shellfish and marine mammals added variety to the diet. Salmon and steelhead were caught in weirs and sometimes speared at night by torchlight. Inland tribes used dogs to chase down deer or run them into snares. If deep snow trapped deer, the Indians killed the floundering animals with clubs. Grizzly and black bears were taken on occasion, particularly if they could be killed while the animals were sleeping in their winter dens. Grasshoppers were even captured by setting fires to grassy hillsides to kill the insects, which were harvested— already roasted. In addition to meat, all these tribes consumed berries, acorns and roots.

Fires were a major influence on the vegetation of this region, and they restricted fire-sensitive species such as mountain hemlock and white fir to the moister sites, while increasing the distribution of fire resistant species. Indians and white settlers also employed fires to clear the landscape or as a hunting tool. The early whites in the Rogue and Applegate valleys also set what were called "light burns," to reduce the build-up of brush and keep forests open for easy horse travel and to aid livestock grazing. In the early 1900s the Forest Service encountered resistance in trying to enforce its fire suppression policy, and the local folks continued to set fires in blatant disregard of federal edicts. The agency even proposed to infiltrate the countryside with spies to capture arsonists. Eventually the Forest Service won out and fires ceased to be a major influence on the region's vegetation. Recent research on the natural role of fire in the ecosystem now shows the early fires may have had a

Gold Beach at the mouth of the Rogue River was the site of a gold rush during the 19th century. Today it survives on fishing, tourism and some logging. GEORGE WUERTHNER

Few of these people lived in large groups, the average village being no more than 40 to 100 individuals. Several related families often occupied houses made from split cedar or pine. Private property was an important part of the culture and individual families typically had reserved hunting and fishing grounds, acorn and berrying sites. In addition, slavery was a common institution and the ownership of large numbers of slaves was a sign of wealth. Since warfare was the principal means of obtaining more slaves, these tribes were unusually hostile, and the French Canadian fur trappers working for the Hudson's Bay Company referred to them as "rogues." The name was adopted for the major river that flowed through the region.

Rush for Gold

Other than an occasional skirmish with the roving bands of trappers, few conflicts between whites and Indians developed until the first major influx of Europeans. This came in the 1850s following the discovery of gold on Josephine Creek, a tributary of the Illinois River. New placer discoveries on Jackson Creek in

1852 precipitated a major gold rush and the creation of the town of Jacksonville. Other strikes soon followed throughout the Siskiyou region, including Kerbyville, Williams Creek, Althouse Creek and the Applegate River. Gold also was taken from the beaches at Gold Beach, Pistol River, Port Orford and Bandon. Battles between the Indians and miners occurred at frequent intervals during the "Indian Wars" between 1851 and 1856, when the tribes were subdued and sent to reservations.

After this the wave of miners created a demand for new trails and roads to haul supplies, thus stimulating further development of the region. The population of Oregon west of the Cascades jumped from 9,083 in 1849, the year before the first gold discovery, to 52,465 by 1860. Much of this population increase can be attributed to the flood of miners and the people who started farms to supply these gold seekers with food.

Among the new arrivals were Chinese miners, who worked for wages since they were not allowed to own mining claims. Orientals were treated poorly and even their murder was not considered a crime. In at least one case on

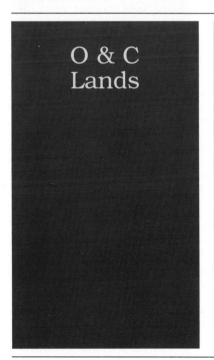

O & C Lands

The railroads became owners of huge tracts of western timberlands through grants of alternate sections (called checkerboard ownership) of public lands along railroad rights of way. More than 131 million acres of public lands (the total U.S. Forest Service holdings amount to only 174 million acres) were ultimately donated to the railroads; some 44 million acres, an amount equal to two thirds of the state of Oregon, were conveyed to the Northern Pacific Railroad alone.

A typical example of this land-grant process was the Oregon and California Railroad land grant (known as O and C lands). In 1866 Congress authorized a grant of 20 sections of land for every mile of construction on the railroad that was to run from Portland to California. The stipulations of the grant required that lands could be sold only to "actual settlers," in tracts no larger than 160 acres, and at prices not to exceed $2.50 per acre. Since most of the land claimed by the railroad was heavily forested, few settlers were interested in buying it, and the railroad began to sell its land for the timber value, which exceeded the $2.50 per acre limit. By 1903 an estimated 85 percent of these lands had been disposed of illegally and in 1916

Congress repossessed more than 2 million acres of the unsold lands. These, together with the Coos Bay Wagon Road lands, which also returned to federal ownership, comprise the O and C lands now administered by the BLM.

Unlike most BLM lands that tend to be unwanted acres of public domain, the O and C lands are very productive and in fact are some of the best timberlands in Oregon. Just as the U.S. Forest Service compensates counties for losses they would have gained in property taxes had all the land passed into private ownership, the BLM arrived at a formula providing affected counties 50 percent of the revenues from the sale of timber, with the rest of the profits going back to the BLM to build more logging roads, for reforestation and to otherwise improve the land for timber harvest. For counties like Josephine, Douglas, Jackson and others in southern Oregon's Siskiyou Mountains, as much as half of the county revenues totaling in the millions of dollars comes from O and C lands. In 1985 the BLM paid out some $117 million to Oregon counties with O and C lands within their borders. Because of the large sums of money involved, the BLM is under tremendous pressure not only from the logging industry to increase its cut, but also from the county commissioners who want to see timber-sale receipts increase.

record a miner who shot a Chinese man in Jacksonville during a drunken spree was found guilty only of shooting a gun within the city limits.

Most large placer deposits were worked with hydraulic mining operations that stripped away the overburden of gravel and rocks with water under high pressure. Miles of ditches and flumes were constructed— for example, the Sterling mine was 23 miles long— usually with Chinese labor, to divert water to the mining project. Large hydraulic operations were used at Waldo, Takilma, French Flat, and Allen Gulch. Hydraulic miners also operated along the Rogue River at Galice Creek and elsewhere.

The miners had a major impact on the region's wildlife. Large animals such as elk, grizzly bear and deer were hunted for food and occasionally hides. Until the turn of the century steelhead and salmon were so thick in the Applegate and other rivers that the miners captured them in their sluiceboxes. These fisheries were destroyed when stream beds were dug up and the siltation resulting from mining activities smothered spawning beds.

In the late 1800s sheep and cattle grazed throughout the high basins of the Siskiyous. In 1903 alone some 103,000 sheep and 7,500 cattle were counted along the crest between present-day Interstate 5 and Highway 199. The mountains were severely overgrazed and still bear the scars of this exploitation.

Commercial fishing followed the gold rush era. The heydays of this industry are probably gone forever, but fisheries remain an important local and regional resource. The major salmon rivers such as the Chetco, Elk, Sixes, Pistol, Rogue, Applegate and Illinois are nearly all wild fisheries and provide the stock for much of the commercial catch all along the Oregon coast and even as far north as Alaska. In addition, once the fish return to the rivers, sport fishing for salmon and steelhead (a sea-run rainbow trout) supports a large guiding and outfitting business on the Rogue and other rivers. In 1986 90,000 spring chinook salmon and 150,000 summer-run steelhead made the run up the Rogue River. In addition, the region's rivers host runs of sea-run cutthroat trout, coho salmon and American shad.

Most of the rivers in the Siskiyous are free of major dams that decimated anadromous fish runs elsewhere in Oregon. But the fish face other problems. The proliferation of logging roads causes siltation of streams, destroying fish spawning sites as well as aquatic insects, which young fish eat. Thermal pollution, or the rise in water temperature associated with low flows in late summer, contributes to many problems for cold-water fish like salmon and trout. As timber is cleared from higher elevations, snowmelt increases on the open slopes so that peak run-off occurs earlier in the year. This leaves less water during the critical late-summer period. But it would be unfair to attribute all fishery problems to logging, for other human activities also affect water levels. Draw-downs for irrigation, and to a lesser extent for domestic water supplies, exacerbate a naturally low water flow that would occur regardless of the human influences. In March, peak flow on the Illinois River at Kerby averages 292,500 acre feet, while in August the average is less than one hundreth the discharge in March— or 2,580 acre feet. Other rivers have similar March maximums with August and September lows.

The best known and most popular river in the Siskiyous is the Rogue. Beginning in the Cascades near Crater Lake the river loops first south, then north, then south again, all the time flowing west to the coast, where it enters the Pacific at Gold Beach. Gold was found here at the river's mouth as well as up and down its steep canyon cut through the barrier of the Siskiyou Mountains. Today thousands of people travel the river in rafts, kayaks and jet boats; others hike the riverside trail through the canyon. In 1968, 84 miles of the Rogue were designated a Wild and Scenic River and a portion of it is also included in the Wild Rogue Wilderness.

Timber Economy vs. Wild Land

Except for the coast, large-scale logging was slow to develop in the Siskiyous. The inaccessible, steep terrain thwarted timber harvest and most of the early efforts of the Forest Service in this region were focused on controlling overgrazing and stamping out fires. With the increase in logging that followed World War II, the timber industry now dominates the local economies of the area. The Bureau of Land Management and the Forest Service have large timber holdings in southern Oregon, and since 1975 the six southern Oregon counties have received $761 million dollars from the federal government in timber harvest receipts paid in lieu of land tax. According to timber industry statistics, some 50 percent of the region's workers are directly or indirectly employed by the forest products industry, hence there is strong pressure on federal agencies to continue the current level of timber harvest. Eighty percent of the timber cut today comes from old-growth forest stands; some economists and foresters predict a shortfall in timber supplies if harvest levels continue at the present pace.

The economy of Grants Pass along the Rogue River gradually is shifting from timber to tourism and services, as retirees and visitors flock to the Siskiyou region. GEORGE WUERTHNER

Facing page: The Illinois River, a designated Wild and Scenic River, flows through the heart of a proposed Siskiyou National Park. GEORGE WUERTHNER

Not everyone is happy about the rapid liquidation of these forests, and environmental groups charge that both the Forest Service and BLM are overcutting their lands and exceeding their own stated sustained yield plans. One area of major conflict has been the 110,000-acre North Kalmiopsis roadless area, located between the Illinois and Rogue Rivers and reputed to have the finest stands of old-growth timber left in southwest Oregon. Conservationists have spent years seeking wilderness status for this area of open meadows, steep mountains and giant old trees, and have even blockaded proposed logging roads. They have had small successes, but each year new clearcuts and roads further shrink the acreage.

The North Kalmiopsis is part of a more ambitious conservation project, the proposed Siskiyou National Park. The park would include all of the Kalmiopsis and Wild Rogue wildernesses along with the designated portions of the Illinois and Rogue wild and scenic rivers. These would be linked together with the 100,000-acre South Kalmiopsis and 20,000-acre Shasta-Costa roadless areas and portions of the Chetco and North Fork of the Smith rivers. Altogether some 750,000 acres of the Siskiyous would be given park status providing an economic resource to the region. For scenery and recreation, the Siskiyous are outstanding. More importantly, it may be one of the few areas in Oregon diverse enough to sustain a functioning ecosystem with a complete complement of wildlife species. Wide-ranging predators such as mountain lions and wolves would find enough territory and prey to survive. It is of sufficient size to allow natural ecological processes such as wild fires, floods, insect outbreaks and population fluctuations to occur without significant interference from humans. If any mountain range in Oregon is deserving of national recognition, it is the Siskiyous.

CHAPTER 9

The Coast Range

Above: Clouds and mist swirl among the gentle, forested ridges of the Coast Range near the Alsea River. Heavy precipitation and a mild climate produce the most spectacular coniferous forests in the nation. Right: In the Coast Range, trees grow right down to the ocean's edge, as here near Cape Foulweather.
GEORGE WUERTHNER PHOTOS

A 1986 survey of state Welcome Center visitors indicated that the Oregon coast was the preferred destination of more than 40 percent of those queried and ranked substantially higher than any other part of the state as their vacation choice. Such a finding is not surprising, for outside of Alaska there are few places in the United States where the meeting of sea and shore is as dramatic. Except for the few strands of sand dunes and wave-cut benchlands, the coastal mountains, hills and headlands seem to fall into the Pacific, and forests of Sitka spruce, Douglas fir and western hemlock cloak the highlands in almost impenetrable tangles of lush vegetation. All but 26 miles of the 363-mile coastline are publicly owned, making this one of the most accessible stretches of ocean-front property in the nation.

The Coast Range extends from the Columbia River on the north to the Coquille River in the south by Coos Bay, and is bounded on the east by the Willamette and upper Umpqua valleys. Below the Coquille to the California border, the geologically different Siskiyou Mountains form the coastal hills abutting the sea. The average height of the Coast Range is only about 1,500', and most of the terrain is more hilly than mountainous. The highest summit in the range is Mary's Peak (4,097') by Corvallis, but several other mountains including Bone Mountain (3,661'), Bald Knob (3,630'), Saddle Mountain (3,283') and Mount Hebo (3,174') also rise above 3,000'. Although in this region of high precipitation, rivers are numerous, only three—the Siuslaw, Umpqua and Columbia— actually cut through the range.

Nearly the entire population of this region is located along the coast itself, and the mountains are virtually uninhabited. A third of the people live in five coastal towns: Astoria, Seaside, Tillamook, Lincoln City and Newport. Tourism, logging, fishing, dairy farming around Tillamook, and retirement living are the chief economic activities of the region.

Mountains Meet the Sea

The Coast Range began to take shape about 35 millon years ago when the sinking seafloor abruptly changed its orientation from a curving line bending northeast from the present location of Eugene to the straight north-south line that we see today. A slab of sea floor that had been moving under the edge of the continental plate was isolated to form what is today the northwest portion of Oregon, including everything north of an imaginary line running from Coos Bay northeast all the way to Pendleton. Sediments from the new sinking seafloor were

Dense forest cover near Mt. Hebo.
GEORGE WUERTHNER

scraped off and shoved under the old slab, wedging up the western edge to create what we call the Coast Range. Since the Coast Range is a chunk of old seafloor, most of the rocks are sandstones, mudstones, and basalts.

Many of the older basalts formed underwater are warty-looking masses. Geologists call them pillow lavas and they are characteristic of the Coast Range. One good place to see them is in roadcuts along the drive to the summit of Mary's Peak outside of Corvallis and at Devil's Elbow State Park north of Florence. Seafloor basalts are extremely resistant to erosion and many of the most spectacular segments of coastline, such as the section from Yachats south to Heceta Head, are sculpted from basalts that were extruded over the ocean floor.

If these pillow lavas are formed close to shore, they may be buried by layers of sediment washed in from the surrounding land, making alternating layers of basalt and sedimentary rock.

Top: Sand dunes at Oregon Dunes National Recreation Area.
Bottom: Lodgepole pine takes a brushy, twisted shape when grown in the nutrient-deficient sandy soils along the coast, hence its Latin name of Pinus contorta.
GEORGE WUERTHNER PHOTOS

Mudstones in the north end of the Coast Range contain many fossil seashells of tropical species, indicating that the climate at one time must have been much warmer. Other rocks in the southern edge of the Coast Range near Coos Bay also were formed under tropical conditions and large swamps must have existed along what was the coastal plain of the Siskiyous. The resultant coal deposits were mined from 1854 into this century, but mining closed down when oil became the dominant source of energy.

A number of rugged headlands such as Yaquina Head and Cape Foulweather are remnants of old volcanoes composed of very hard, erosion-resistant basalts. Seal Rock is another basalt remnant. Waves wash against the shore, eroding the softer sandstones surrounding these basalt rocks, leaving them as sea stacks and headlands.

South of Florence, sand dunes dominate the coast all the way to Coos Bay. These shifting dunes are formed when sand, moved up on the beach by waves, dries and is blown inland by the stiff offshore winds; grains of sand pile up to create some of the most extensive coastal dunes in the country and are now part of the Oregon Dunes National Recreation Area. The coastal mountains just east of the dunes are composed primarily of sandstones that formed on the seafloor and provide a source for new sand as rivers slowly wash them into the sea.

The Coast Range was not high enough to support glaciers during the last Ice Age, and thus lack U-shaped valleys and cirques characteristic of glaciated regions. While many of the higher peaks have rounded summits, the stream-cut canyons are often deep and steep-sided. Since rainfall is heaviest on the coastal side of the mountains, stream erosion has cut deeper into the western slope of the range than the eastern side and the main watershed divide is much closer to the Willamette Valley than the coast.

Because of the heavy rainfall, much of the ancient bedrock is weathered and subject to mass slippage. Sedimentation from landslides has increased dramatically as logging, and the access roads associated with it, have destabilized slopes. Many harbors require constant dredging to remain open, and coastal estuaries, important nurseries for fish and waterfowl, are filling rapidly under the unnaturally heavy silt load. One study found that landslides in roaded drainages were 25 to 340 times greater than in unroaded drainages. Another found that landslides due to roading often do not occur until triggered by particularly big storms. This research project found that the landslides did not take place until seven years after the road construction.

A Climate for Making Trees

Heavy rains are the norm as moisture-laden air from the ocean moves inland. The air masses abruptly collide with these coastal highlands, and in rising to cross over them the air cools and releases great quantities of water on the western slope. Some coastal areas experience more than 180 days of measurable precipitation a year. Valsetz, for example, receives an average of 126" of precipitation annually. Astoria on the north coast averages 11" of precipitation per month during December and January, while the July average is only an inch of precipitation. The ocean also moderates the temperature extremes. Winters are extremely mild; Astoria's record low was 10 degrees and Newport's one degree. Summers are cool, particularly for areas within a few miles of the shore. Although summers are typically dry, fog is common on the western slopes of the mountains throughout the season.

The mild climate with heavy winter rainfall feeds one of the lushest temperate coniferous forests in the world. The largest Sitka spruce in the United States grows six miles south of Seaside on private timberland. The giant measures 52' 6" in diameter and is 700 years old.

Besides Sitka spruce, the most common tree species are Douglas fir and western hemlock. The spruce dominates sites close to the ocean, while Douglas fir is most abundant inland. Western red cedar and grand fir are frequently intermixed with these other species, while noble fir is found at higher elevations in a few areas from Mary's Peak northward. In the understory of these forests grow shrubs such as red huckleberry, rusty menziesia, vine maple and a variety of ferns and herbs.

Lodgepole pine is a common species on sandy soils near the coast. This coastal variant looks like an entirely different tree from the same species east of the Cascades or in the Rockies. Few coastal pines have the tall, slender boles of the inland variety, but instead are shrubby, broad-crowned and short. David Douglas, the botanist for whom Douglas fir is named, was the first to give lodgepole pine its scientific name of *Pinus contorta*, which means twisted pine. The only representatives of the species that Douglas had seen were the specimens growing along the Pacific Northwest coast. The common name, lodgepole, refers to the Rocky Mountain variety, which grows straight with very little taper. It is ideal for framing Indian teepees, or lodges, and hence its name.

Conifers dominate the region because they can withstand the summer droughts better than hardwoods, which are restricted to riparian zones. The most common hardwoods are bigleaf maple, red alder, willows and black cottonwood. On many exposed hillsides along the coast are open meadows called headland prairies. How they developed or why they persist is not fully understood but they probably were created by a combination of factors such as high winds or past fires. They are often covered with grasses, herbs, bracken ferns and shrubs like salmonberry and wild rose.

Old Growth Forests

The old-growth coniferous forests of the Pacific Northwest, stretching from southern Alaska to northern California, are among the largest living entities in the world with a complex of interrelationships to rival the much-heralded tropical rainforests. Our own temperate rainforest consists of giant Douglas firs reaching heights of 250' or more, and having an average diameter of eight feet. Equally large species include Sitka spruce, western red cedar, Port Orford cedar, and of course the even larger coast redwood. Based on average height alone, there are no comparable forests on earth.

These conifer timberlands are unique among temperate forest regions of the earth. Most temperate zone forests are hardwoods or some mix of conifers and hardwoods—as in the eastern United States, Japan, China and northern Europe—but here, as nowhere else on earth, grow the most magnificent coniferous forests in the world.

The definition of old growth is somewhat nebulous. There is no specific age at which a forest becomes "old growth"; rather, it depends upon physical characteristics. Old-growth forests tend to have a layered, multistructural appearance with tall old trees towering over younger trees of varying age classes. Snags and broken-top trees are abundant and fallen logs litter the forest floor. In short, this is the kind of forest that generations of foresters have learned to call decadent, sick and unproductive.

New research has found that these supposedly unproductive and decadent forests are the key to a healthy ecosystem. The large, dead logs that litter the floor of old-growth forests are long-term structural components of the ecosystem and as important a resource as the trees growing above them. The useful life of a log goes many years beyond the time it was alive. As a fallen log on the forest floor it has another, perhaps even more important, role in the forest ecosystem than when it stood upright. It takes 300 or 400 years or more for fallen trees to completely rot and recycle into living matter, hence fallen logs provide long-term nutrient stability to the ecosystem.

On the forest floor, large fallen logs soak up moisture during the long winter rains. Then during the characteristic summer drought of the Pacific Northwest, these logs often provide the only source of water available to seedlings, and even to mature trees. Another unappreciated benefit of old-growth forests may be their ability to reduce the frequency and extent of wild fires. Fires have trouble burning through a damp forest floor covered with large, water-logged, fallen trees. Old-growth forests serve as natural fire breaks in the ecosystem and normally do not burn except under the most extreme fire conditions. Thus, they serve as refuges from the blazes and help to maintain islands of uneven-age forest amid the sea of new growth that comes in after a burn.

Large fallen trees also provide stream-bank stability in small and medium-size streams by helping to dissipate the erosive energy of flowing water. The sheltered nooks and pools created around these massive barriers also provide important fish habitat, and studies have shown a correlation between the abundance of dead, fallen material in and alongside streams and the productivity of fisheries. In small streams nearly 50 percent of the fish habitat is created by fallen trees. Even after a major catastrophe such as a forest fire, the remaining dead snags often fill a stream with debris that preserves fish habitat for hundreds of years, until the new forest grows up to replace this resource. The liquidation of the old-growth forest, and its replacement with young, small trees cut in rapid succession on a rotational basis, eliminates these massive structures and destroys a resource—large fallen logs—which we are not replacing, or planning to replace.

In addition to the structural roles that large trees play in the forest environment, there are a host of intricate plant-animal, plant-plant, plant-soil associations. Nearly all trees and higher plants act as hosts for plants called mycorrhizae, which means "fungus root." Mycorrhizal fungi attach themselves to the roots of plants and form tiny hair-like rootlets that assist plants in the absorption of nutrients and water. In exchange for this help, the plants provide mycorrhizomes with food. Neither can survive very long without the other.

Mycorrhizae not only form interdependent relationships with plants, but with animals also, as exemplified by the California red-back vole, which lives under large fallen trees. Nearly 75 percent of the vole's diet consists of truffles (the reproductive equivalent of seeds) of mycorrhizal fungi. After eating these plant parts the vole acts as dispersal agent when it distributes the spores in its feces. The vole needs the mycorrhizal fungi for food, while the mycorrhizae need the transportation services of the vole. In addition, the vole needs the trees to provide the large logs that are its preferred habitat. This is only one of thousands of similar interlocking cogs in the typical old-growth forest.

View north of the Coast Range from its highest point on Mary's Peak near Corvallis.
GEORGE WUERTHNER

How much old growth is left depends upon whom you ask and how old growth is defined. Conservationists claim that fewer than 10 percent of Oregon's forests are still in the old-growth category, and most of this number are in the Cascades. The Coast Range has less than 2 percent old growth and the large-boled, mature ponderosa pine forests east of the Cascades are also fast disappearing.

Old-growth forests are being liquidated at an alarming rate. The acreage of old-growth Douglas fir in the states of Washington, Oregon and northern California has shrunk from 15 million acres at the time of settlement to 5 million acres today, and most of this has been cut since 1950. If these remaining forests could be collected in one spot, they would equal only twice the size of Yellowstone Park. There is virtually no old growth left on private timberlands, although at one time these holdings had the largest percentage. All that remains is found on public lands. At the present time 80 percent of this old growth, or some 4 million acres, is scheduled for timber harvest in the next few decades. On many national for-

ests in Oregon and elsewhere, virtually no old-growth Douglas fir will survive outside designated wilderness areas or other special reservation zones.

No one knows how much old-growth forest is necessary for long-term ecological stability; researchers estimate a minimum of 30 percent — yet many national forests already have slipped far below this level. For example, the Siuslaw National Forest has only 3 percent of its forests left as old growth, and the Coos Bay district of the BLM, which encompasses some 330,000 acres of extremely productive timberlands, will have only 33,000 acres of old growth by 1990, or less than 10 percent.

How much old growth is enough? Probably all we have left and then some. One Oregon conservation group has proposed that all the remaining patches of old growth be designated a national monument to preserve a part of the state's heritage — large trees, which the members believe equal in importance to scenic areas such as the Columbia Gorge and Crater Lake.

Left to right:
Moss-strewn maple struggles for light in the Drift Creek Wilderness. Old-growth forests typically have a multi-layered structure not found in even-aged second-growth forests.
Giant old-growth Sitka spruce, like this in the Rock Creek Wilderness, are becoming rare outside designated wilderness and national parks as timber harvest removes the last stands of these magnificent giants.
Clearcut on the Siuslaw National Forest. GEORGE WUERTHNER PHOTOS

In spite of the generally wet climate, some of the largest wildfires in Oregon burned through coastal forests before the advent of modern fire suppression. The Tillamook Fire, really three separate fires, burned more than 350,740 acres of the northern Coast Range in 1933, 1939, and 1945. The lush climate allows fuels to build up so that during an especially dry summer, fires burn with unstoppable intensity.

As might be expected with a dense cover of valuable trees, logging has been, and continues to be an important part of the economy of coastal communities. A good portion of the Coast Range is privately owned by timber companies, while there are also state-owned forests, BLM timberlands, and the Siuslaw National Forest. Almost all the privately owned lands have been logged and no old-growth timber remains on them; even a good portion of the public lands has been roaded and logged. For instance, in 1980 85 percent of the Siuslaw National Forest was already developed, logged and roaded. For all intents and purposes the Siuslaw is totally given over to timber harvest. Even the back side of the Forest Service Research Natural Area at Cascade Head has been cut over. Clearcuts drop down to the shoulders of main highways and to the edges of residential areas. The trees are apparently too valuable to leave as hedgerows for aesthetic purposes. If any part of Oregon is a tree farm, this is it. Douglas fir and Sitka spruce are the the primary timber species and the largest mills are at Wauna, Astoria, Warrenton, Tillamook, Toledo and Coos Bay. Today less than 3 percent of the Coast Range forest consists of old growth and nearly all of this is on public lands. More timber has been cut than reforested, and as a consequence the logging industry, already on the skids, may slump further once current supplies are exhausted.

Logging began in the Coast Range shortly after the discovery of gold in California increased the demand for timber products in the West. One of the first mills was built at the mouth of the Umpqua River in 1864. Oxen dragged the logs to the river and the timber was floated to the mills for sawing. Sawn lumber went under sail to California markets.

The light, strong wood of Sitka spruce was an important structural component of airplanes during World War I, and towns like Toledo boomed. After the war, logging waned until World War II, and in the post-war years the demand for wood products continued.

Three small wilderness areas occupy less than 1 percent of the land area in the Coast Range. All three of these—Drift Creek, Rock Creek and Cummins Creek wildernesses— offer a glimpse of what the unlogged, old-growth coastal forests were like. Cummins Creek Wilderness is the largest at 9,019 acres, yet is only seven miles long. The Drift Creek Wilderness has centuries-old trees festooned with moss and lichens. Vine maples grow in small forest openings, looking like delicate trellises as their branches weave through the forest for extra light. When I visited these three areas sign of Roosevelt elk was everywhere in evidence.

In addition to these wilderness areas and the state parks, an Oregon Coast Hiking Trail has been proposed, which would run from the Columbia River to the California border, following beaches, passing over headlands and leading through the patches of remaining old-growth forests. Portions of this trail are already in place and each year new mileage is added.

Trails are actually a new phenomenon for the coast as the original settlers and the Indian tribes, both of whom lived in small villages aligned primarily at the mouths of the rivers, traveled by canoe. Early explorers to the coast noted that many of these aboriginal people had deformed and crooked legs, they presumed because of the great deal of time spent squatting in the cramped confines of a canoe.

People of the Coast

Whether they actually had deformed legs from sitting in canoes is open to speculation, but many coastal tribes purposely flattened their children's skulls for cosmetic reasons. Strapped into a wooden cradle just after birth with a cord or tightly plaited grass wrapped around a board applied across the forehead, the child was kept in its cradle for four to eight months until the bones of the skull had deformed into the new shape. A child who was not deformed in such a manner could never gain status or respect within the tribe.

Rich food resources including berries and vegetables, salmon, shellfish, whales, seals, and land animals such as deer and elk were available.

The bald summit of the Coast Range near Mt. Hebo is slowly revegetating after large fires, collectively called the Tillamook Burns, swept over the region during the 1930s.

Facing page, left: Darlingtonia, an insect-eating pitcher plant, grows in a cedar bog near Florence.
Right: Waterleaf in the Drift Creek Wilderness.
GEORGE WUERTHNER PHOTOS

A lush growth of ferns along Drift Creek. GEORGE WUERTHNER

Among these coastal tribes status was accorded to individuals who had the most possessions, which were given away at ceremonies called potlatches. The distribution of gifts brought great esteem and recognition. Warfare was the usual means by which an individual obtained wealth, which included slaves. A man with many slaves held great status and achieved a leadership role in village affairs. One way to show respect for and impress a visiting dignitary was to kill a number of slaves and place them under the visitor's canoe as it was beached, so that its surface never came in contact with the shore.

Clothing was minimal and almost all coastal natives went barefoot year-round. In extremely wet weather, a poncho-like raincoat made from bark was often worn, along with a woven hat that shed water. Most household items and structures were made from wood, and elaborate buildings were erected, often with decorative ornaments. Villages consisted of one or more large wooden houses, constructed of planks laboriously split from large trees like cedar. These structures housed two or more families, often related, and a village usually consisted of no more than seven or eight of these houses.

Canoes were carved from a single tree and its construction was a major project. Cutting down the tree before the introduction of steel axes was a time-consuming proposition, accomplished by burning a fire at the base of the selected tree and tending it for days until it had eaten completely through the wood. The boat builders hollowed a shallow trench with stone adzes, and fires were set inside the fallen log to burn away the wood. Eventually, as the canoe took shape, the canoe was filled with water heated with hot rocks, to make the wood pliable. Poles were knocked into place to stretch apart the sides and enlarge the opening. The launching of a new canoe was an important affair and one or two slaves would often be sacrificed to christen the boat.

Indian names are common along the coast and include Neahkahnie Mountain, named for a deity that turned to stone. Siuslaw means "far away waters" and was the name of a tribe of Indians that lived along the river. Other prominent coastal features were named by early explorers sailing the coast in the 1700s. Cape Perpetua was named in 1778 by Captain James Cook, an English explorer, who supposedly named the headlands when bad weather stalled him in the same location and the cape was perpetually in view. Cape Foulweather was also named by Cook when the weather was particularly unpleasant. One gets the impression that Cook did not enjoy his voyage along the coast.

Despite the many sailing vessels that traveled the coast during these early years, all of them missed the mouth of the Columbia River. It was not until 1792 that the American trader, Captain Robert Gray, sailed through breakers at the river's mouth into one of the greatest western waterways discovered by Europeans. Gray named the river for his ship, the *Columbia.* Gray's discovery of the river and the early land-based travels of Lewis and Clark and other Americans laid the basis for American claims to the Oregon Territory. Of course, these claims ignored the Indian's prior occupation.

Lewis and Clark were the first whites to venture overland into what would later be Oregon. They arrived in 1805 by way of the Columbia River and spent the winter at their tiny Fort Clatsop near present-day Astoria. The expedition suffered through a winter, wracked by boredom and made miserable by the cold, wet weather. They even complained about their food which they described as "tasteless elk meat." The entire crew was happy and relieved when they began the homeward trek on March 23, 1806.

Based on the Lewis and Clark explorations, traders began to go overland to Oregon to tap its rich fur resources. In 1811 John Jacob Astor's trading party, called the Astorians, built a fort and trading post at the foot of Coxcomb Hill. The fort was captured by the British during the war of 1812 and eventually operated by the British Northwest Fur Company. It returned to American hands in 1818 and became an American settlement thereafter, retaining the fort's name of Astoria.

The fur-trading era did little to disturb the Coast Range, for travel through the dense forests was difficult and trapping success was limited. Along with logging, fishing was one of the first industries in the region. Nearly all the coastal rivers once supported runs of salmon and steelhead, and the Columbia was probably the largest producer of anadromous fish on the entire west coast. It is estimated that Indians, fishing with spears, nets and baskets, were able to harvest 18 million pounds of fish a year.

Commercial fishing began in an important way during the 1880s and 1890s. Without the technology to freeze fish, the catch had to be preserved quickly, so canneries were built near the major fisheries up and down the coast and along the Columbia River. Thousands of boats were involved in the harvest so that overfishing took its toll and the catch eventually declined.

To add to the problems created by overfishing, dams on the Columbia and its tributaries began to make inroads

on the salmon runs. Migrating fish had difficulty ascending the fish ladders, and not all dams were equipped with them. The young fish suffered high mortality on their downstream journey when they passed through the chopping blades of the hydro-electric turbines. The fishing industry suffered further decline as logging increased substantially after World War II. A recent Oregon Fish and Game report concluded that half the anadromous fish habitat in the Coast Range was destroyed by logging operations. The huge runs of silver fish that used to jam many coastal streams are things of the past, but both commercial and sport fishing still draw people to the coast.

Tourism is the only growth industry along the coast and accounts for a large percentage of the economy. Lincoln County had the second highest level of tourist-related

employment and second highest income derived from tourist-related travel in the state. The ease of public access to both mountains and beaches, combined with the many state parks, campgrounds, motels and other facilities have aided the travel industry. As the mountain watersheds recover from the disastrous effects of logging, fishing may improve and help balance the region's economic base. But, the coast's real gold mine is its scenery, beginning to be tapped and representing a resource that will never be exhausted if care is given to protect the landscape from unwise development.

Left: The bold headlands of Cape Foulweather are composed of erosion-resistant basalt.
Right: According to Oregon Fish and Game estimates, sedimentation from timber harvest has reduced anadromous fisheries along the coast by 50 percent, crippling the state's fishing industry.
GEORGE WUERTHNER PHOTOS

CHAPTER 10

Basin and Range Mountains

Saltgrass among salt deposits by Borax Lake, Alvord Desert.

Abert Rim, a 2,000' fault scarp, is typical of the Basin and Range province. GEORGE WUERTHNER PHOTOS

143 miles long by 86.6 miles wide and bigger than any one of the eight smallest states, had a 1985 population of 7,350 with 60 percent of this total concentrated in the towns of Burns and Hines. Except for the occasional ranch and dirt road, most of southeast Oregon is more remote and untamed than what pass as wildlands in the state's officially designated wilderness areas. These wide, open spaces of sage flats, rimrock and alkaline lakes seem like a wasteland to many as they drive by on lonely roads like Highways 395 and 95. Yet, as in any landscape, there is a beauty to be found for those who take the time to explore. Impressions linger: the fresh scent of sage after a summer thundershower; the white rump flash of a startled antelope as it speeds across the hills; and the quiet solitude of a land unpeopled, where hawks, jackrabbits and cattle still dominate the countryside.

Fault Block Mountains

The Basin and Range province of Oregon is the northwest corner of a much larger geographical region that covers most of Nevada, parts of Utah, California, Idaho, New Mexico and Arizona. The term Basin and Range refers to the large-scale vertical displacement of the earth's crust, generally in a north-south orientation, that creates what are known as fault-block mountains. These ranges are separated by wide basins— usually with no external drainage. Oregon's portion of the province occupies much of the southeast corner of the state and is bounded by the Cascades to the west and the Owyhee Uplands to the east, while the High Desert Lava Plains mark its northern limits.

There are a number of mountain ranges and isolated ridges within the area including Steens Mountain, Pueblo Mountains, Trout Creek Mountains, Sheepshead Mountains, Abert Rim, Hart Mountain, Warner Mountains, Winter Ridge, Gearhart Mountain and other isolated peaks, hills and rims. Most of these uplifts are characterized by a steep face along the fault zone, such as the 2,000' scarp of Abert Rim seen along Highway 395 north of Lakeview. Most of the valleys are at 4,000' while the highest individual peaks are Steens Mountain (9,733'), Pueblo Mountain (8,634'), Hart Mountain (8,065'), Beatys Butte (7,916'), Gearhart Mountain (8,364'), Drake Peak (8,402') and Crane Peak (8,454').

Most of the region is extremely arid and dominated by sagebrush, grasslands and dried-up lakebeds known as playas. Only the higher elevations and riparian zones

Mule deer tracks and frosted junipers at Drinkwater Pass. The Basin and Range province typically has hot, dry summers and cold winters.
LARRY ULRICH

Left: The rugged eastern face of Steens Mountain drops more than 5,000' in fewer than three miles to the floor of the Alvord desert below.
GEORGE WUERTHNER

From my camp on the summit of Steens Mountain I watched the sun slip below the western horizon and the stars begin to dot the heavens. As twilight turned to darkness, tiny pin-pricks of light flicked on across the vast reaches of southeast Oregon, each marking an isolated ranch or house. From my lofty perch I could see east beyond Juniper Mountain and west of the Sheepshead Mountains to the Owyhee country— perhaps 60 or 70 miles in either direction— yet in that entire region, only eight lights indicating human habitation were visible. I knew a few more ranches were hidden behind the rugged rimrocks and canyons before me; nevertheless, it is indeed true that one can see many more stars in the night sky above Oregon's Basin and Range province than lights in its valleys. The population density of this portion of Oregon is 0.8 people per square mile— even Alaska's 1.4 persons per square mile is greater!

Most of this geographical region is public land— Bureau of Land Management (BLM), Wildlife Refuge, and Forest Service— with population centers few and far between. Harney County, which includes Steens Mountain and is

Top left: Saltgrass along the edge of Soap Lake in the Pueblo Valley, with the Pueblo Mountains beyond.
Top right: Ancient shorelines from Ice Age lakes are visible like a bathtub ring on the slope of Poker Jim Ridge at the Hart Mountain Wildlife Refuge.
Above: Borax Lake chub, found only in Borax Lake, is able to tolerate extremely salty conditions.
GEORGE WUERTHNER PHOTOS

have any trees. But the mountains along the western fringe, closer to the Cascades, such as the Warner Mountains and Gearhart Mountain area, are heavily forested with conifers and the ranges to the east may have a limited forest cover, if any at all. These include the Trout Creek Mountains, Pueblo Mountains, Sheepshead Mountains, Steens Mountain and others.

One would not be incorrect in generalizing that all of Oregon's Basin and Range mountains are exposed blocks of basalt or rhyolite. Huge basalt floods covered southeast Oregon and are thought to be of ages similar to those of Columbia River basalts found farther north. Nevertheless, the "Steens basalts" differ in composition and can be identified by their large crystals of feldspar, which give these dark rocks a streaky appearance. In some parts of the province, deposits of rhyolite, a light-colored volcanic rock, indicate that the upward-moving basalt passed through continental rocks like granite. The granite melted and mixed with the basalt to create the lighter-colored rocks. Geologists believe the presence of rhyolite indicates that the former margin of the continental plate is buried beneath the more recent basalt and rhyolite flows. Further evidence is found among the granite boulders exposed in the Pueblo Mountains south of Fields, which are similar in age and composition to rocks of the Blue and Siskiyou mountains. The rocks in the Pueblo mountains, and nearby Trout Creek Mountains, are the

only major outcrops of non-volcanic rock found in all of southeast Oregon.

The Steens basalts were formed some 15 million years ago when layer after layer (75 distinct layers have been counted) of fluid rock erupted from long fissures or cracks in the earth's crust and spread out for miles over the land. In addition to these ancient flows, volcanic activity continued on and off to the present. One of the more spectacular areas of recent volcanic eruptions is the Diamond Craters region south of Malheur Wildlife Refuge. Few regions of the United States can rival its diversity of volcanic features— such as craters and cones— within so small and accessible an area. Other volcanic landmarks include a collapsed caldera, the Whitehorse, found in the Trout Creek Mountains and eroded volcanic spires in the Gearhart Mountain area.

Thin-Skinned Earth

Although volcanic activity has been recorded during historic times, much of the region is still underlain by hot magma extremely close to the surface as indicated by the abundance of hot springs that dot the region. A drilled well at Crump acts like a geyser and erupts at 80-minute intervals. Other hot springs are found at Hart Mountain, below Steens Mountain, and north of Lakeview. Mickey Hot Springs, on the flanks of the Sheepshead Mountains, is one of the hottest in the region, reach-

ing temperatures of 210 degrees and featuring mud pots and steam vents.

Borax Lake, in the Alvord Desert, is fed by 97-degree hot springs and its clear waters feel like a lukewarm pool— a refreshing place to swim if the day is not too cool. Other nearby springs have deep, scalding hot and translucent blue waters like the glory hole hot springs found in Yellowstone National Park. Minerals (sodium borate) in the thermal springs precipitate out along the lake margin, creating natural levees. Around the turn of the century a mining company worked the area commercially. These white crusty deposits were added to water and the mixture was boiled in huge vats. Acid was later added and boric acid was crystallized out of the mixture. Four hundred tons of refined borax were hauled 130 miles by 16-mule-team wagons to Winnemucca, Nevada for shipment on the railroad.

Despite the warm, salty waters, Borax Lake is home to the Alvord chub, a fish no more than four inches long, found nowhere else in the world. The Nature Conservancy has been conducting population studies to determine the current status of this unusual species.

The original basalt floods created a relatively level plateau, but fractures of the earth's crust have uplifted, dropped or tilted huge blocks to create the mountains, rims and valleys we see today. Steens Mountain is

an example of such a fault block uplifted 5,500' above its eastern base. Today the mountain's western flank rises at a 3-degree angle across an 18-mile-wide slope, while the steep eastern face drops at a 20-degree angle from its summit to the base in fewer than three miles. Other obvious fault-block mountains include Hart Mountain, Pueblo Mountains, Winter Ridge and Abert Rim.

Sometimes a portion of the earth's crust drops between two faults, creating a valley rimmed on both sides by cliffs, which is known as a graben. The Alvord Desert basin and the Warner Valley below Hart Mountain are bounded by grabens.

During the Ice Age glaciers covered Steens Mountain and perhaps Gearhart Mountain and Drake Peak. Although the latter two areas were barely touched by glacial erosion, Steens Mountain has perhaps the most visible and dramatic glacially carved features in the entire state. Due to the lack of screening vegetation, gorges like the Kiger, Big and Little Indian, Little Blitzen and Wildhorse offer textbook examples of U-shaped glacier-carved valleys. Numerous cirque amphitheaters lie along the crest of the range, and several glacially-carved lakes, including Wildhorse Lake, dot the uplands.

Glaciation was limited in southeast Oregon, but the wetter climate during the Ice Age resulted in the formation of numerous large lakes that filled most of the basins of

Top left: Glaciers once covered all of Steens Mountain and carved deep U-shaped canyons and cirque lakes like Wildhorse Lake. GEORGE WUERTHNER Top right: Little Blitzen Gorge, a glacially-carved valley on Steens Mountain. LARRY ULRICH Above: Glory Hole hot spring in the Alvord Desert. GEORGE WUERTHNER

93

Above: Reeds in Malheur Wildlife Refuge south of Burns.
Right: Lichens cover volcanic boulders in the Trout Creek Mountains.
GEORGE WUERTHNER PHOTOS

the region. Goose, Abert, Summer, Harney, Malheur, and the lakes strung along the Warner Valley are all remnants of much larger water bodies that existed thousands of years ago. Old shorelines, visible as terraces at the foot of mountains, mark the former high-water mark of these Ice Age lakes— good examples of ancient beachlines can be seen along the west slope of Poker Jim Ridge at Hart Mountain Wildlife Refuge and along the Catlow Rim. In recent years higher than normal precipitation has resulted in the formation of a lake in the Alvord Desert basin and has expanded Malheur Lake, which has risen by seven feet and now inundates thousands of acres of ranchland that had been settled during years of low precipitation. Since many of these ranches border the Malheur Wildlife Refuge, there is discussion of the government's buying the flooded lands and expanding the refuge borders.

The flooding at Malheur is the result of short-term weather disturbances, but over all the region is known for its aridity. This region is typically referred to as Oregon's eastern desert, and in terms of climatic data, the appellation is appropiate. The driest recording station in Oregon is at Andrews, a small ranching hamlet below Steens Mountain where the average annual precipitation is a mere 7". Andrews rests in the "rain shadow" of Steens Mountain, which blocks moisture-carrying air masses from the west, but even Burns, located north of Malheur Wildlife Refuge in an open valley, receives only 12" of precipitation a year. The climate can best be termed as harsh, but healthful: hot, dry summers and cold, dry winters. The minimal precipitation comes primarily as snow and during infrequent summer thundershowers.

But these averages vary more here than elsewhere in

Big sagebrush exemplifies some of these adaptations. Its leaves are small to reduce the area exposed to high temperatures and they are covered with tiny hair-like pubescences that help to reduce evaporation losses. In addition, when soil moisture is high during the spring, big sagebrush produces deciduous leaves, which it drops once the summer drought season begins, leaving behind smaller, evergreen leaves throughout the year. Big sagebrush also possesses an hourglass-shaped root system with two concentrations of roots. A branched tap root draws on deep water sources, and a network of shallow roots just below the surface takes advantage of surface moisture. The aromatic odor we associate with sagebrush is actually a chemical defense that makes it difficult for both insects and wildlife species to digest the plant's leaves.

Contrary to popular thought, sagebrush probably was always an important feature of the region's vegetative community and did not suddenly appear as a result of overgrazing, for the pristine plant communities were a mix of sagebrush and grasses like bluebunch wheatgrass and Idaho fescue. Nevertheless, these grasses have been replaced on thousands of acres by the non-native invader cheatgrass and less desirable native grasses like Sandberg's bluegrass. In many areas sagebrush has increased substantially from its pre–livestock-grazing densities.

The higher elevation reaches of the western Basin and Range mountains, including Winter Ridge, the Warner Mountains and the headwaters of the Sprague River around Gearhart Mountain, are heavily forested with giant old-growth ponderosa pine, white fir, whitebark pine, lodgepole pine and some of Oregon's most extensive aspen groves. Meadows and forest-rimmed openings are common.

Although the western mountains are covered with coniferous forests, the more arid eastern ranges often lack any trees at all. Because of the distance from potential sources of colonization, many species common elsewhere are absent from suitable habitat here. For instance, the only conifers found on Steens Mountain are two small 50-acre patches of white fir— and the only other tree species found here is aspen. In a similar fashion, Hart Mountain boasts aspen groves and small patches of ponderosa pine in five west-slope canyons, along with a few white fir, but no other kinds of trees. Aspen, along with narrowleaf cottonwood— a species that reaches its northwest distribution here— are the only trees in the Pueblo Mountains.

Old-growth ponderosa pine at Bull Prairie in the Warner Mountains. Mountains of the western portion of the Basin and Range province are well forested.

Left: Extensive alpine grasslands cover the long summit ridge of Steens Mountain.
GEORGE WUERTHNER PHOTOS

Oregon. For example, the record high for Andrews is 107 degrees, while the low is a frigid 33 below zero. And year-to-year variation is tremendous; Burn's average of 12" was topped by 17" in 1940 and cut in half in 1937 when only 6" fell.

Plants and Animals Adapt to the Desert

Many of the plants and animals living in this part of Oregon have some adaptations for coping with the aridity and temperature extremes. Lower and middle elevations are dominated by drought-resistant shrubs such as big sagebrush, silver sage, saltbrush, bur sage, greasewood, juniper, mountain mahogany and various grass species including great basin wild rye, Sandberg's bluegrass, cheatgrass, bluebunch wheatgrass, bottlebrush squirreltail, Indian ricegrass, Idaho fescue and crested wheatgrass.

Sunset over Upper Campbell Lake at Hart Mountain Wildlife Refuge.
GEORGE WUERTHNER

Islands of Isolation

Since these Basin and Range mountains are like islands separated from other plant sources by miles of inhospitable desert, genetic isolation has produced many species endemic to the region and plants with unusual distribution. Steens Mountain alone sports 30 species that are considered of special interest, including lance leaved grapefern, Cusick's horsemint, Sierra spring beauty, arctic willow, dwarf birch, Steens Mountain thistle, moss gentian, wedge-leaf saxifrage and Steens Mountain paintbrush. Other mountains also contain significant plant populations. Both the Trout Creek Range and Pueblo Mountains have five plant species listed on the state's Rare, Threatened, and Endangered Species list: red buttercup, two-stemmed onion, thick-leaved phacelia, nodding melic, and ochre buckwheat.

Some of the most beautiful and extensive subalpine and alpine plant communities in the entire state are found on the rolling plateau-like summit of Steens Mountain. The grasslands are dominated by sheep fescue and rough fescue along with many low prostrate flowers—including lupines, buckwheats, buttercups, cinquefoil, yarrow, locoweeds and Oregon silene. In the wetter basins and cirques a profusion of wildflowers blooms during the short summer months, including bluebells, bistort, shooting stars, marsh marigold, steer's head, false solomon's seal, false hellabore and monkey flower.

But plants are not the only species isolated by the islands-habitat phenomenon. The redband trout, a form of rainbow trout adapted to warm temperatures and alkaline waters, spread throughout southeast Oregon via the large glacial lakes that existed at the close of the Ice

Age. Then, once the lakes dried up, this trout was left isolated in the tiny creeks and rivers that nose their way down from the mountains. Confined to small streams, these trout seldom attain large sizes, and a 12" fish is considered a giant. Another Ice Age relict, the Whitehorse cutthroat trout, is known only from two small creeks in the Trout Creek Range, but has been transplanted into suitable habitat in both the Pueblo Mountains and Steens Mountain area to increase its range.

As with plants, many mammals, particularly those found at lower elevations, are adapted to aridity. In this part of Oregon one may encounter typical desert species such as Ord's kangaroo rat, white-tailed antelope, ground squirrel and the kit fox. On the high-elevation islands of moist habitat are animals like the pika, a small rabbit-like animal common in the Rockies and Cascades, but found only on Steens Mountain in this part of Oregon.

Two of the most ubiquitous species are the black-tailed jackrabbit and its major predator, the coyote. Both animals are much maligned and bounties once existed for both of them. In 1915 Harney County paid five cents each for 1,029,182 jackrabbit scalps before deciding control-by-bounty was too expensive. While no coyote bounty exists at present, they are still killed for their hides or predator control. In 1986, 167 coyotes were trapped or shot on Malheur Wildlife Refuge alone. But both jackrabbits and coyotes are fecund species and control is short-lived.

Steens Mountain, a large isolated mountain island of habitat more typical of mountain ranges farther north, once supported the wolf, lynx, wolverine and grizzly bear. A lone wolverine was reported on the mountain in 1975, but these animals are wide-roaming, and this sighting probably does not represent a breeding population. Although elk have recently colonized Steens Mountain from the north, they were not known to inhabit the mountain in pre-settlement times. Elk have also recently colonized Hart Mountain, moving in from the Warner Mountains to the west.

As the early trappers and explorers who first left records of wildlife distribution and numbers testify, southeast Oregon never had huge wildlife populations. If lacking in numbers, many species were widespread. For example, nearly all the mountain areas had populations of California bighorn sheep. Because of competition from domestic livestock, introduction of diseases, and hunting, bighorn sheep disappeared from all their historic ranges in this region. Bighorns were reintroduced to Hart Mountain and they now number 400 to 600. Descendants of

the Hart Mountain herd have been reintroduced throughout the state. At present, 250 to 300 bighorns roam Steens Mountain, some 175 sheep are found in the Pueblo Mountains and another 50 summer on Alvord Peak and migrate out into the Alvord Desert to winter. The most common large mammal likely to be seen, particularly at lower elevations, is the antelope, which was once almost eliminated from the state. Protection has brought their numbers back to approximately 15,000 animals. Although usually found in the valleys and flats, antelope occasionally roam quite high in the Trout Creek Range, on Hart Mountain, and on Steens Mountain they have been seen above 9,000'. Antelope are typically associated with open, treeless terrain, but one antelope herd has an unusual habit of moving west from lowlands near Winter Ridge through heavily forested terrain to slopes of the Cascades by Crater Lake where they summer in a ponderosa pine-bitterbrush habitat.

Yet, in spite of the aridity, concentrations of wildlife can be spectacular. Malheur Wildlife Refuge is a haven for waterfowl and birds like the sandhill cranes, trumpeter swans, and a variety of raptors. Hart Mountain National Antelope Refuge, established in 1936, protects spring, summer and fall ranges of antelope and also the largest bighorn sheep herd in Oregon. The numerous lakes in the Warner Valley just below the Hart Mountain escarpment are also a major waterfowl and bird sanctuary.

Tough People in a Tough Land

It was just such wildlife concentrations that supported a small population of Northern Paiutes. At the time of white contact, this Shoshonean-speaking, desert-dwelling tribe had moved north from Mexico to exploit the limited resources of southeast Oregon. Because of the widely distributed, seasonally available food, these people had to move frequently. The most common social organization was a man and his wife or wives, their children and perhaps a grandparent or two. Almost everything was a possible meal including roots, berries, seeds, cattail pollen, grasshoppers, lizards, snakes, waterfowl eggs, fish and beetles. Occasionally several families gathered for animal drives. Jackrabbits, an important Paiute food species, were captured with nets set in suitable habitat. Young boys drove the animals toward the nets where they were clubbed to death by the waiting hunters. Although big game such as deer, antelope and bighorn sheep were taken on occasion, small animals such as ground squirrels, rabbits and waterfowl provided most of the meat.

Above: Red-band trout from the Trout Creek Range.
Top: Twisted bole of aspen at Hart Mountain, one of the few tree species found in southeastern Oregon's mountains. GEORGE WUERTHNER PHOTOS

Cheatgrass and rabbitbrush and the typical upthrusted slope of fault-block mountains of the Basin and Range are seen here near Blizzard Gap. GEORGE WUERTHNER

Fremont, with Kit Carson as a guide, journeyed south along the east side of the Cascades and passed over Winter Ridge along his route. Fremont named the mountain for the bad weather he had on its summit, while he named the lake below, Summer Lake, because the sun was shining on its green, grassy shoreline. The Fremont National Forest by Lakeview was named for this wide-ranging surveyor.

Few people ventured into the region until the 1860s when Army troops were stationed at various camps throughout the region to protect travelers, most bound for the gold fields of northeast Oregon or Idaho. A number of battles between troops and Indians occurred and by 1868 the Indian resistance was broken. With the threat of attack controlled, ranchers began to invade the area to take advantage of grasslands that once blanketed the interior basins and slopes.

Conquest by Cattle

The first permanent settler was a Californian, John Devine, who settled on Whitehorse Creek in the Trout Creek Mountains. He brought with him 3,000 head of cattle, Mexican vaqueros, and a large herd of horses to begin a cattle empire. Devine loved race horses, fine wines, and entertaining guests with gourmet foods in his remote kingdom that soon included most of the Alvord Basin. Then a series of droughts dried up the springs, wet meadows disappeared, and grass productivity declined. Devine's cattle starved and his operation went bankrupt in 1889. Another cattle baron, Henry Miller, bought Devine's property and retained him as manager, giving him the 6,000-acre Alvord Ranch fully stocked with cattle for his own, which he operated until his death in 1902.

Another legendary cattleman was Peter French, who once had a cattle empire of 45,000 head and 150,000 acres of land. Like Devine, French came from California leading 1,200 head of cattle, along with horses and a few Mexican vaqueros. Backed by a wealthy Sacramento Valley landowner, Dr. Hugh Glenn, French established a ranch on the Blitzen River below Steens Mountain and eventually came to own ranches from the Catlow Valley to Malheur Lake. (The town of Frenchglen commemorates these two partners.) As more and more people came into the region, French increasingly had disputes with his neighbors over land ownership, water rights and grazing rights. One of these squabbles led to his death in 1897 when an angry neighbor shot French after they had quarreled.

But even as skillful as these people were at exploiting the food resources of the region, starvation was common and some had to resort to cannibalism to survive lean times.

The first whites to penetrate southeast Oregon were members of a Hudson's Bay Company trapping brigade led by Peter Skene Ogden, who made four trips through the region from 1825 to 1828. Ogden caught beaver, like the Paiutes, but he found big game scarce and his party was often hungry. In 1831, another Hudson's Bay employee, John Work, passed what is today known as Steens Mountain. Work called the high, long ridge "Snow Mountain," but the name was later changed to Steens for Major Enoch Steen, who chased a group of Indians across the mountain in 1860.

Other trappers wandered through the region, but the next notable exploration was conducted in 1843 by Captain John Fremont, of the Topographical Engineers.

Domestic sheep were brought into the region shortly after the first cattle ranches developed and soon outnumbered cattle. But unlike most cattlemen, sheep herders seldom bothered to set up a home ranch. Instead they moved their flocks over the open range from high summer ranges to the desert lowlands for the winter. By 1900 an estimated 140,000 sheep grazed the highlands on Steens Mountain alone. With the depredations of the sheep and cattle, rangelands were severely overgrazed and many have not recovered to this day. Unfortunately, past and present negative impacts from livestock grazing are still widespread on public lands throughout the region despite 50 or more years of range management.

Evidence of range abuse includes: trampled stream banks; loss of riparian vegetation like willows; the widespread loss of desirable grass species like Indian ricegrass and bluebunch wheatgrass and its replacement with undesirable grasses like cheatgrass; soil compaction which speeds run-off, causing gullying and a subsequent drop in the water table; pedestal plants, which indicate soil erosion. Overgrazed ranges can be found on Steens Mountain, in the Warner Mountains, in the Pueblo Mountains, the Gearhart Mountain Wilderness, Trout Creek Mountains, the Sheepshead Mountains and even within wildlife refuges like Hart Mountain. The decline in range productivity due to livestock overgrazing probably has as much to do with the agricultural crisis since many more acres are needed to support each cow than was necessary when the first cattlemen like John Devine wandered into these valleys.

Although the desert country is probably too arid and the grass cover too sparse to profitably ranch without a good supply of hay meadows, it is an even poorer place to try farming. Yet homesteaders flooded into the Oregon desert after the turn of the century, enticed by several years of above-average rainfall and the lure of free land. Small towns with names like Sageview dotted the dry valleys and the settlers tried to raise wheat on the dusty playas of ancient lakebeds. The Catlow Valley, for example, had a population of 700 people, but the "wet" years soon turned dry and by the 1920s most of these farmers had given up in despair, leaving shanties and old fences to mark their efforts.

Today cattle ranching still dominates the landscape and livestock are more numerous than wildlife on both private and public lands, even on wildlife refuges and within designated wilderness. For years the public lands have been used as if they were privately owned rangelands,

Pinnacles of volcanic rock along Trout Creek in the Trout Creek Mountains. GEORGE WUERTHNER

but in recent years interest has heightened in their suitability for other resource uses and concerns. The BLM, which administers most of the public lands in southeast Oregon, is presently conducting wilderness suitability studies for its roadless lands throughout the state. Some of the largest and most spectacular proposed wilderness areas are found in this region. Among the areas being considered for wilderness classification are: the Hart Mountain-Guano country, the Sheepshead Mountains, Steens Mountain, Pueblo Mountains, Abert Rim, Trout Creek Mountains, Poker Jim Ridge, Basque Hills and Catlow Rim.

A Steens Mountain National Preserve is an objective of some conservationists, but as yet no formal proposal for its protection exists. It would include the entire mountain and perhaps the adjacent Alvord Desert. This exceptional scenic area, coupled with the wildlife attractions of Malheur Wildlife Refuge, would make an impressive drawing card for southeast Oregon's budding tourist

Public Lands Livestock Grazing

Livestock grazing is one of the most widespread and dominant uses of the public domain, particularly in eastern Oregon. As such, it has a direct impact upon many other resources including watershed, wildlife and recreation. Of the millions of acres of Bureau of Land Management (BLM) lands in eastern Oregon, nearly all are under grazing lease. For instance, of 3.6 million acres on the Burns BLM district, 3.5 million are leased for grazing and similar figures are available for other BLM districts. On the Burns district 64,429 cattle and horses and 685 sheep are grazed by permit each year, and 279,785 animal units per month (AUM) were allotted to livestock. Yet on the same district only 8,347 AUM's were allotted to wildlife. On the Vale BLM district the figures are 573,529 AUM's to livestock and 12,961 to wildlife. Such lopsided allotments can be found on all public grazing lands including national forests and even designated wildlife refuges.

These are obvious conflicts and impacts, but many others are more subtle. Cover and nesting habitat for many bird and mammal species is destroyed by trampling and the changes in plant composition that often accompany heavy livestock grazing. Comparisons of ungrazed land and those used for livestock production at Malheur Wildlife Refuge have shown a decline in duck nesting success, passerine (primarily songbird) bird populations, and hawk utilization of habitat in all areas managed for livestock.

Grazing may also be a factor contributing to the current decline in sandhill crane populations, since evidence shows that grazing (and mowing) removes cover, increasing losses due to predation. Rather than decrease livestock grazing, Malheur Refuge personnel poisoned ravens, trapped raccoons, and shot 167 coyotes in 1986. Crane numbers have been on a severe downward trend and perhaps predator control was necessary, but it seems ironic that on a wildlife refuge, wildlife was killed before grazing controls were attempted. Actual grazing levels at Malheur were increased in 1986.

Riparian zones are usually the richest and most diverse wildlife habitat available, particularly in the arid eastern mountains, providing water, shelter from sun and wind, and a variety of plant foods. But more than any other topographical feature these are the areas most devastated by livestock. On the Burns BLM district in eastern Oregon 69 percent of the

Left to right: Erosion on Steens Mountain, likely the result of overgrazing by livestock. Elimination of cover by grazing at Malheur Wildlife Refuge has hurt some wildlife populations on the refuge. Cattle trails on steep hillsides.
GEORGE WUERTHNER PHOTOS

riparian zones were in poor or fair condition and only 7 percent were in a climax or excellent condition. As streamside vegetation such as willows disappears due to grazing and trampling, banks collapse and stream downcutting increases with an eventual drop in watertables and the loss of wet meadows. Everything from nesting passerine birds to big game suffers from the loss of cover and nesting habitat.

Many riparian areas grazed by livestock show substantial fish population declines. Usually the grazed creeks are shallower and wider, while ungrazed streams are deeper and narrower. A study on the Little Deschutes River found trout populations were 350 percent higher in ungrazed than grazed portions of the river.

It might be assumed that public lands grazing continues because it is profitable to the government, but such is not the case. Ranchers pay a token fee ($1.35 per AUM) for utilizing nearly all grazeable public land, including wilderness areas and wildlife refuges, but these fees are well below their actual market value and do not come close to covering the costs of managing rangelands, much less mitigating the damage done by livestock.

For example, in 1985 the Oregon BLM spent $4,777,653 on range management and improvements, yet only collected $1,298,782 in grazing fees. Low fees are one rea-

son the BLM and other agencies lack the funds to adequately monitor range condition and to properly protect sensitive areas like riparian zones from grazing impacts.

These are the direct costs attributed to livestock grazing programs, but there are many other hidden costs such as the esthetic costs, which include miles of overgrazed and beat-up rangelands, polluted water, and "cowed out" camp sites that are never figured into the cost of public land grazing.

Ironically, only two percent of the red meat produced in the United States comes from western rangelands, and Florida with its wet, highly productive year-round grazing produces more meat than all the western states combined. Even though eastern Oregon is thought of as cowboy country, the arid climate and sparse vegetation require immense acreage to support one cow and few operations would be profitable without the subsidies provided by public-land grazing. With milder, wetter climate and rich soils, the predominantly private grazing lands of western Oregon support more domestic sheep and nearly as many cattle as the lands east of the Cascades. There is no reason to eliminate all public-land grazing, but conservationists are calling for a shift in priorities—from favoring livestock to protecting and nurturing wildlife, watersheds and recreation.

Alvord Desert from Steens Mountain.
LARRY ULRICH

trade. An even more ambitious plan calls for a National Ecological Preserve that would include all of southeast Oregon and adjacent parts of Idaho and Nevada. Management of this immense region would be directed toward restoration of species diversity and of natural ecological communities and processes. This would require the acquisition of strategically located private lands through purchase or trade, dramatic reductions in livestock grazing on public lands, reintroduction of extirpated species, and the reestablishment of natural processes such as wildfire, insect outbreaks and floods.

No matter what direction public lands management takes, the mountains of Oregon's Basin and Range province will likely remain for a long time a place where antelope outnumber people and the eye can sweep uninterrupted across a hundred-mile horizon.

OREGON'S HIGHEST PEAKS

The following is a list of Oregon's higher peaks divided by geographical regions. The list is representative of each major mountain area, but does not necessarily include all the high peaks found in each geographical subdivision. This is a revision of geographical facts originally published by the University of Oregon in the *Atlas of Oregon*.

Name	Elevation in Feet
CASCADES	
Mount Hood	11,245
Mt. Jefferson	10,497
South Sister	10,358
North Sister	10,085
Middle Sister	10,047
Mt. McLoughlin	9,495
Mt. Thielsen	9,182
Broken Top	9,173
Bachelor Butte	9,065
Diamond Peak	8,744
Bailey	8,363
Aspen Butte	8,208
Pelican Butte	8,036
SISKIYOU MOUNTAINS	
Mount Ashland	7,533
Dutchman's Peak	7,418
Grayback Mountain	7,055
Lake Peak	6,642
Craggy Mountain	6,331
Rustler Peak	6,208
Soda Mountain	6,091
Brandy Peak	5,316
Pearsoll Peak	5,098
Chetco Peak	4,660
COAST RANGE	
Mary's Peak	4,097
Bone Mountain	3,661
Bald Knob	3,630
Saddle Mountain	3,283
Mount Hebo	3,174
Roman Nose	2,856

Name	Elevation in Feet
BLUE AND WALLOWA MOUNTAINS	
Matterhorn Peak	9,845
Sacajawea	9,839
Aneroid Mountain	9,702
Petes Peak	9,675
Glacier Mountain	9,600
Eagle Cap	9,595
Red Mountain	9,555
Elkhorn Mountain	9,202
Strawberry Mountain	9,038
BASIN AND RANGE MOUNTAINS	
Steens Mountain	9,733
Pueblo Mountain	8,725
Crane Mountain	8,456
Drake Peak	8,407
Gearhart Mountain	8,364
Deadhorse Rim	8,210
Beatys Butte	7,916

Top: Mt. Hood
STEVE TERRILL
Bottom: South Sister
GEORGE WUERTHNER
Facing page, top: Phlox in Crater Lake National Park
STEVE TERRILL
Bottom: Strawberry Falls in Strawberry Mountain Wilderness. GEORGE WUERTHNER

ABOUT THE AUTHOR
Based in Missoula, Montana, George Wuerthner has been employed as a university instructor in California, a surveyor in Wyoming, a ranger and packer in Montana, a wilderness ranger in Alaska and a botanist in Idaho. Between jobs he has backpacked, skied, canoed and kayaked extensively in wild places, taking wilderness journeys of up to four months' duration. His writing and photography have appeared in many outdoors publications.

Oregon Economic Development Dept.
Tourism Division
595 Cottage St. NE
Salem, OR 97310

Oregon State Parks and Recreation Division
525 Trade St. SE
Salem, OR 97310

Oregon Department of Fish and Wildlife
506 SW Mill
Portland, OR 97208

Oregon Guides and Packers Association
Box 3797
Portland, OR 97208

Rogue River Guides Association
Box 792
Medford, OR 97501

Bureau of Land Management
Oregon State Office
Box 2965
Portland, OR 97208

Regional Forest Service Office
Pacific Northwest Region
319 SW Pine St.
Portland, OR 97208

U.S. Fish and Wildlife Service
500 NE Multnomah
Portland, OR 97232

Oregon Natural Resource Council
1161 Lincoln St.
Eugene, OR 97401

Hart Mountain Wildlife Council
Box 111
Lakeview, OR 92630

Malheur Wildlife Refuge
Box 113
Burns, OR 97720

Crater Lake National Park
Box 7
Crater Lake, OR 97604

Deschutes National Forest
211 NE Revere Ave.
Bend, OR 97701

Fremont National Forest
Box 551
Lakeview, OR 97630

Malheur National Forest
139 NE Dayton St.
John Day, OR 97845

Mt. Hood National Forest
2955 NW Division St.
Gresham, OR 97030

Ochoco National Forest
Box 490
Prineville, OR 97754

Rogue River National Forest
Box 520
Medford, OR 97501

Siskiyou National Forest
Box 440
Grants Pass, OR 97526

Siuslaw National Forest
Box 1148
Corvallis, OR 97330

Umatilla National Forest
2517 SW Hailey Ave.
Pendleton, OR 97801

Umpqua National Forest
Box 1088
Roseburg, OR 97470

Wallowa-Whitman National Forest
Box 907
Baker, OR 97814

Willamette National Forest
Box 10607
Eugene, OR 97440

Winema National Forest
Box 1390
Klamath Falls, OR 97601

A Study in Oregon, Its Beauty, Its People

Next in the series

WESTERN OREGON:

Portrait of the Land and its People

GEORGE WUERTHNER

What makes Western Oregon so alluring, so distinctive? Why does it look the way it looks? What do all these people do? This is the one book that documents in straightforward text and stunning photography the essence of all of Western Oregon—not just the world-famous coast line or the dominating beauty of the Cascade Range. It describes the entire region by its natural features—weather, landform, the direction its waters flow, its vegetation and wildlife. And it becomes a dialog with the people about their communities, about their lifestyle along the coast and in the mountains. Conversations with Western Oregonians reveal the special urbanity of the cities of the Willamette Valley tempered by all that beautiful surrounding country and help us understand the economy driven by its natural resources. This is Western Oregon seen from an eye in the sky, as well as from across the coffee table.

About the Oregon Geographic Series

This series is your guide to enjoying and understanding Oregon's places, people and landscapes.

Color photography of the interesting and unspoiled country of Oregon illustrates every book, and each text is written especially for this series to help you explore, experience and learn about this fascinating state.

Write to:
American Geographic
  Publishing
P.O. Box 5630
Helena, MT 59604
(406) 443-2842

Please send suggestions for titles you would like to see in the Oregon Geographic Series and your comments about what you see in this volume.